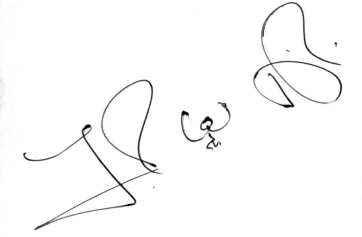

Also by Frank Dick

Sports Training Principles
Winning
Winning Lines

Winning Matters

Frank W Dick

First published in Great Britain 2010
Reprinted 2011 and 2012

A CIP catalogue record for this book is available from the
British Library

ISBN: 978-1-872317-04-5

Printed and bound by CPI Group (UK) Ltd, Croydon, CR0 4YY

*To everyone who stood me on their shoulders
to help me get a different view of the world.*

ACKNOWLEDGEMENTS

Sometimes it is more from listening to how a question is worded than in an answer given. Sometimes it is more in how someone has perceived my words when I thought I'd said something else. Sometimes it is in a briefing, sometimes in a de-briefing; or it's a line in a film, a moment in an arena, lateral thinking connected or a simple observation. But always it's something I have learned that I would never have come up with entirely by myself.

I acknowledge then, and with deepest gratitude all those who have provided the 'sometimes' in shaping what I needed to learn to write this book. If I had to list all, that would need another book. It would probably amount to everyone I have ever spent time with. In particular, however, I would like to mention those who, far more often than I could have reasonably expected of them, chose to lend a patient listening ear and afford wise counsel whether I was in their areas of expertise or off track. They gave me the ideas, all I had to do was write them into these pages.

Peter Godfrey, Andy Cross, Malcolm Brinkworth, Roger Moreland, David McWhir, Paul Campbell, David Moulsdale, Neville Pritchard, Alan Finlay, Sue Peters, David Sheepshanks, Caroline McHugh, John Bales, Dean Benton, Ian McGeechan, Sue Campbell, Pat Duffy, Lorraine Lafreniere, Andy Roxburgh, Harald Spiegel and Bill Sweetenham. Then of course, there is the inner circle, Linda, Erin and Cara. They gave me true perspective in all things. Jamie helped there too!

Finally, a very special thanks to Anne Farrow who translated my handwriting into readable text; Wendy Robinson for an excellent editing job and Geoffrey Hamilton-Fairley for having faith in me to deliver a sequel to 'Winning'.

INTRODUCTION

Whatever you do in life it is almost inevitable that your performance is assessed. To perform you need two basic attributes that when combined and developed make you a winner:

- A desire to achieve
- A set of skills in order to be able to achieve

Some eighteen years ago I wrote 'Winning'. I did so because I found myself addressing audiences who wanted to know if the skills and motivation from sporting achievement could be successfully translated into performance within the business environment. I know from very positive feedback that the coaching concepts and motivational tips conveyed in presentations and subsequently in 'Winning' have made a difference. Since writing 'Winning' I have spent many hundreds of hours consulting, presenting and conducting workshops in varied sectors of business and finance. Apparently, I have spoken to over 500,000 business men and women during the past twenty years. I believe that I now have a greater and in depth understanding of the challenges faced when attempting to win in the business arena at all levels. The skills required are in some ways more subtle than those required in sport, so in this new book 'Winning Matters' I have honed the sporting paradigms and analogies to reflect this.

I also wanted to build on the structure of the original

book which was designed for busy productive people whose time is precious. Both books are structured for you, the reader, to dip in and pick up a motivating quote or thought in a few seconds, easily explore more detail of that particular topic in a few minutes and should you desire, expand to associated topics. I hope that every time you pick up 'Winning Matters' it brings something positive to your day.

CONTENTS

Contents

COACHING TO WIN

To achieve beyond our individual isolated capabilities we need others – we all know this but it is difficult and complex to achieve in reality. True winners fly towards their mountain range of hopes and dreams on the horizon, trusting a colleague to be the wind beneath their wings that lifts them higher to go the distance. Then next, they are the wind beneath their colleagues' wings to speed them on their journey.

It is as if each of us is like a player-coach. One moment we are coachable, soaking up the lessons of our life experiences and coached by those who will make sure the lessons are not only learned but translated into action. The next moment we are passing on what we have learned and coaching those who need our help to be different, to be better, to win.

You would expect me to introduce coaching early in 'Winning Matters', because that's my life. In fact, I have an incredible passion for coaching, fuelled by the many coaches who have influenced my life, or whose work I have studied. Not all of the people I would call my coaches would consider referring to themselves as such. Of course there are those whose hard work and wisdom received scant return in the shape of my performance as an athlete! But, like you, there were my parents, teachers, bosses, colleagues, friends and indeed anyone whose advice and support we respect as being offered with only one purpose in mind; to help us be the person we each need and want to be. They coach us to be winners in the sense set out in Chapter 1. There is a process to this because coaches take us from a point where we are dependent on their input and guidance to being interdependent by being a player coach, learning faster together with other player coaches than on our own. Chapter 8 goes through this process in detail. Coaches empower us to take *ownership* of winning, of turning the experience of each moment in our life journey into an opportunity to be better.

Sometimes coaching is about learning how to exercise good judgement to be most effective in our *decision making*, to add quality to our life and to the community to which we belong within the framework of rules that shape our behaviour and culture. Sometimes coaching is learning skills, being fit and tactically wise; or about competing within the accepted rules. We are coached in what to *do* to be excellent in executing our role according to these rules or when the rules are changed. The theme of **O**wn, **D**ecide, **D**o is threaded throughout the book. It is a behavioural triad which I believe underpins performance excellence from beginner to the most senior level in all organisations. It makes winning a probability.

Coaching is of course a learning conduit, so naturally, learning is another recurrent theme. Chapter 5 stresses the importance of preparing to learn fast through regular review and monitoring. Chapter 10 looks at building performance from getting the basic skills right through seven learning steps to winning again and again. A critical aspect of planning and preparation concerns creating the environment that makes it possible for us to perform at our best. Chapter 9 examines this as a role of management to leverage practical advantage from what we learn.

Our lives are definitely not like merry-go-rounds in a

fun fair. They are more like white knuckle rides where we must be prepared for change and to change. Chapter 2 describes change as the game we must win. We know that we must make every moment count not only for us but for our colleagues. We also know we must make it count for those who will follow. For each person, whatever their role in an organisation, in order to **O**wn, **D**ecide, **D**o, they must reflect the culture of the organisation.

Just as our coaches built roads and bridges through what was for them uncharted wilderness so that we would have a better life than they, so must we for the next generations. That means not only making a winning difference for the moments around us now, but having the courage to face major issues like culture change when we know that having started the process of change we may not see it completed in our time. We must therefore develop and apply our leadership skills to greater effect as discussed in Chapter 3, and grow to be the leaders we must be to create change. Making the right decisions as set out in chapter 4 is the hallmark of quality leaders. The most important decisions we make as leaders are in selecting and developing the people in our teams. Chapters 6 and 7 bring to the table coaching points on these issues.

Once we have learned and coached our people to have all the skills and fitness to address the challenges that face us; once the strategies and game plans are in place and we understand the roles of everyone, then we must **O**wn, **D**ecide, **D**o and be equipped with the mental toughness that separates the winners from the almost rans. Chapter 11 considers this area and sets the scene for Chapter 12 which looks at who you really are, then at the badge you are part of and which is a part of you. The badge may, for example, be the flag that your performance sees raised to the top of the gold medal flag pole, or the brand name that you have helped to increase its market share. It is who you represent and work for. It is who represents and works for you. It is why you dig deeper to fight for the win.

The purpose in writing 'Winning Matters', is to add its content to the input of your coaches and of all other influences that make you the winner you are. It is as much about raising questions as offering advice. And whether it provides challenges or reinforcements, I hope it strengthens your will to be all that you are capable of becoming so that you touch the top of every mountain you set your heart on reaching.

Chapter 1

WINNERS WIN

Winning is about the performance that gets you to the top of your own mountain, then seeking an even tougher one to climb. While you are not always in total control of results or outcomes, you are in total control of your performance. Focus on that and you are a winner.

Make the Moment Count

Whatever your arena, your objective is to win. You have successfully come this far in your life by persistently meeting that objective. In each arena, the consequence of winning can come in every imaginable and unimaginable form and context. It might, for example, be an Olympic gold medal or World Championship; overcoming adversity; making a relationship work better; hitting a business target; passing an exam; living your values; living one more day. You know the challenges in your arenas.

And you win because you understand that it is not only about what you must do to win, but how you do it. So you fight for the win by the rules 'doing things right' and by the framework of your values 'doing the right thing'. People who want to win every now and then are not winners. People who want to make winning their way of life are.

The best of the winners will be those champions whose performance repeatedly redefines excellence.

Winners make the choice of committing their energy, talents and passion to seeking and seizing winning advantage every moment not only in the arena, but in preparation for it. Such moments are everywhere. Each represents at the very least an experience we can learn from and at best it is the turning point in our endeavour. They can be in general lifestyle; in training and practice; and in doing things under pressure. They may be in individual or collective challenges; or in the quality of assisting, complementing, supporting or putting someone else in a position to deliver their role excellence. In some arenas it may even be in providing that final touch which brings the crowd or audience rapturously to their feet!

Winners know these moments are in them and all around them. So what they think; what they do; how they behave, is brought to bear to make every moment count: all of them. What winners cannot know is which moment will become the winning difference. So each is visited with personal excellence.

I guess this was behind a program of error analysis which Ross Brawn bought to training programs during testing for the F1 Pit Teams in Ferrari and now in Brawn GP. It is also behind the All Blacks' fining of players for ball handling errors in pressure training sessions. Practicing bringing skill excellence to every moment in the arena means a greater chance of turning them to winning advantage.

Winners, then, choose to have a winning attitude. They know they cannot always choose or change the conditions and circumstances in their arena, but they can always choose or change their attitude. No one else can choose the winner's attitude. It is your choice to be a winner. You choose your attitude.

Winning Ways

That attitude is reflected in the behavioural triad introduced in 'Coaching to Win' and which will be discussed in more detail in Chapter 10. They **O**wn, **D**ecide, **D**o.

Own
Winners step up to the plate intuitively. They understand the collective purpose and their role within the enterprise. They take control of the moment and seek to turn it to advantage in pursuit of that purpose. They see no obstacle in seizing the moment. They find a way, pausing neither for invitation nor permission.

Decide
They read the situation fast and call the shot. Having owned the moment, they own the decision on how best to leverage it. They lead the solution process of what is to be done, who will do it and how.

Do
They are action people. They just do it! And they do it with that professional edge which separates delivering excellence from doing enough.

I have worked with a number of entrepreneurs, from those who are on the foothills of building small businesses to those in the sky - touching mountain tops of international markets. Each lives an own – decide – do mindset. No matter what our role in our arenas, these three behaviours shape a winning outcome.

Winning is being better today than yesterday – every day.

Frank Dick

If you don't stand for something, you fall for anything.

Don Shula[1]

If you never try, you never know.

Daley Thompson[2]

To win without risk is to triumph without glory.

Pierre Corneille[3]

Winning is

During my time as Scottish National Athletics Coach I used to travel around Scotland, visiting the local athletics tracks to work with coaches. Every now and then kids would come and watch and I remember one day one of them asked if I would coach her. As I mentioned in my introduction to the reprint of 'Winning', this particular girl was nine and wanted to sprint. I worked with her for a month or so and she went to her first 100 metres race lining up with another seven girls. She finished eighth in eighteen seconds. 'I was last' she cried. 'No you weren't, you were eighteen seconds' I said. 'You smashed the twenty second barrier! And you were a whole second faster than I thought you would run. This is your lifetime best, your own personal record! And in some ways you are a first'. 'What do you mean?' 'Well, you are the first athlete I've coached to run eighteen seconds for the 100 metres!'

Two weeks later she had another 100 metres race. What did she now think winning was? Right - beating eighteen seconds. Now, this is where I think we really begin to understand what winning is. Winning is being better today than yesterday – everyday. Some might suggest that this is impossible. I don't agree, because most of us face, not one but a number of different challenges every day. Your performance may not let you achieve the result you want in all of these challenges, but it certainly will in most.

Your life is not like a single lane road. It is more like a three lane motorway (figure 1). The outside lane is your career, profession, occupation. The middle is the family, friends, community, the relationship lane. The inside is you, your identity, your wellbeing. In travelling on that motorway, if anything is not quite right in one of the lanes, the others are compromised. So all three lanes must be in good shape to ensure you travel well. This will be the goal when you pursue and deliver better performance in each of these lanes every day. This is what it takes to be a winner. You can do it. Once again, the choice is yours.

Figure 1

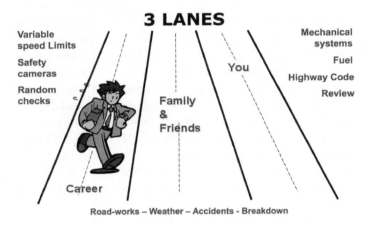

3 LANES

Variable speed Limits

Safety cameras

Random checks

You

Mechanical systems

Fuel

Highway Code

Review

Family & Friends

Career

Road-works – Weather – Accidents - Breakdown

The Winning Difference

There is a popular misconception that the difference between achieving a winning result, or not, is huge. This is not true. It is the consequence that can be enormous. For example, the difference between a gold or silver medal result can mean millions of dollars. The performance difference, however, is incredibly small.

At the Beijing Olympics, USA's Michael Phelps accomplished the extraordinary feat of eight swimming gold medals in one Olympics. He became an icon, he delivered a wonderful moment in sport history. The scale of this might be appreciated on reflecting that the entire USA track and field team achieved only seven gold medals! If he had only collected seven gold medals, it would certainly not have been bad, but, after all, Mark Spitz (USA) had achieved that in swimming back in 1972. Good, then, but hardly history making and certainly not unique. If he had only collected six, well, what a disappointment, because we all knew he was aiming for eight! What was the difference between producing a wonderful moment in history and being a disappointment?

In the 4 x 100 metre freestyle, Phelps had already contributed his 100 metre swim. Jason Lezak (USA) swimming in the final leg, five metres from the finish was trailing Alain Bernard (France) who won the individual 100 metres freestyle event. Lezak touched the wall 0.08 second ahead to give Phelps and the team gold. In the 100 metres butterfly, Phelps was behind Milorad Cavic (Serbia) 50cm from the finish, and touched the wall 0.01 second ahead of his rival to win. So the difference in performance between a moment in history or being a disappointment was 0.09 second. Very few reflexes are that fast!

That's the winning difference. Sometimes you make the difference; sometimes having played your part, it is your colleague who makes your difference count. Winning, then, is about your own performance. Your performance is something over which you have total control. You do not have total control over results. Even a lifetime best may not produce the result you seek, but in my opinion, it is still a win.

John Walker (New Zealand) in 1974 at the Christchurch Commonwealth Games broke the existing 1,500 metre world record in the final. Unfortunately, Filbert Bayi (Tanzania) broke it by more! Now that may be a bummer for John but hardly a failure. To go beyond anything you have done before – that's what winning is. Everything else is a consequence. Or think of it this way, if everyone of us, in a given field or endeavour, improved our personal performance, do you think we have a better chance of achieving the collective result we seek than if we all underperformed? Simple stuff this!

But let's get back to my young Scottish athlete. Soon she is fighting with other athletes to get to the line first. Some would say surely now winning is beating the other girls. Not if she is doing so in nineteen seconds, or we are ignoring our definition of winning!

Challenge Breeds Performance

You see, the reason you go into tougher and tougher arenas is because it is the only way you can improve your performance. You cannot learn to run faster by running against slow people! And none of us can learn how to take on those toughest arenas facing us in the tomorrows ahead if we do not take on the tougher ones now. If we avoid mountains, how can we contemplate climbing our own Everest? You cannot learn to climb mountains by going round them. Rather, we seek out the challenges and the tough stuff, otherwise we are not winners.

And she keeps going until one day that athlete is a one and only. The truth is she always was a one and only just like you. I'll explain why. I have two daughters, Erin and Cara, and am very proud of what they have achieved. As is often the case, when they were teenagers, they stumbled sometimes on their journey to adulthood and we had occasional 'one-to-ones'. You know what I mean! At the end of one of these, I finished in a way that caused each of them to say 'Daddy, if we ever have these conversations again – always say that, because it keeps things right'. Maybe this will keep things right for you:

*'You are the best in the world at being who
you are. Don't ever try to be someone else,
just better at being you. And you will always
touch your mountain tops.'*

When you get things right there is a very real sense of fulfilment, achievement and, in many cases, consequent recognition and even reward. There is also, of course, a persistent sense of challenge in that perfection remains just beyond reach. When you think you are almost there, you must redefine it. Like heading for the horizon, today's perfection is only the end of what you can perceive. It is the start of going beyond to where your imagination will take you. Your constant pursuit of personal performance excellence means your focus is not on what has happened up till now – whether good or not so good: that's history. Nor is it on what the future outcome might be: that's a mystery. It is entirely on *this* moment. It is on what you do and how you do it *now*. When you add up all these moments of performance excellence, the win is yours and the results become more probable. Some hard liners would say that this is all a bit fluffy. It might fit for that young Scottish athlete – but not for the real world of toughest competition.

Well let's look at one of the most incredible Olympic gold medal winning performances ever; the Beijing men's 200 metres track. At the 100 metre mark Usain Bolt was in the lead running 9.96 seconds for the bend. That in itself was pretty incredible as it was the fastest first 100 metres of all time. As far as the other seven runners were concerned the race for gold was now over. In fact, I think Bolt could have hopped the rest of the way and still won gold!

But his race was not with those runners. They were not his benchmark in this race. Nor was the world record,

Don't be afraid to take a big step if one is indicated; you cannot cross a chasm in small jumps.

David Lloyd George[4]

Winners take the risk of winning because they know there is no such thing as risk of losing.

Frank Dick

You were born to win, but to be a winner, you must plan to win, prepare to win, and expect to win.

Zig Ziglar[5]

Those who persist in going beyond enough; who fear neither discomfort nor pain; who will not give in; are practising winning.

Frank Dick

because any sprinter will tell you it is impossible to judge that and, in any case, the experts would have seen Michael Johnson's 19.32 in the 1996 Atlanta Olympics as beyond Bolt's reach. The benchmark for Usain Bolt was himself. The will to fight all the way to the line was etched in his face. He, as with all winners, needed no other person to measure himself against. He was his own pacemaker running 9.34 for the second 100 metres! The gold, and the world record of 19.30 were consequences of the real win which was in delivering his performance excellence. And that was all the more remarkable given that there was a wind against the sprinters of 0.9 metres/second!

One year later at the IAAF World Championships in Berlin the story continued. Having already reduced his own Beijing world record in the 100 metres from 9.65 to 9.58 he again would challenge his personal definitions of excellence in the 200 metres. At 100 metres he recorded 9.92 seconds then produced 9.27 seconds for the second 100 metres and a new world record of 19.19 seconds. He lives the winning definition and he has even more unleashed potential. Sub 19.00 seconds is a real possibility.

Winners are

Winners know their arena and the challenges they represent. They know what's needed to address each challenge successfully and ensure they are prepared through planning, training and practice to deliver the performance to do so, seeking coaching advice and support where necessary. Then they deliver.

Winners test themselves constantly to practice their winning attitude. Ron Dennis, Formula 1's McLaren team former Chairman and Team Principal, challenged himself to park his car perfectly first time at the team headquarters car park in Woking when arriving there every morning. If he didn't he'd punish himself by driving out of the car park and then returning to do it again until it was perfect. Daley Thompson, Olympic and World decathlon champion and record holder brought competition into every aspect of his life. On one occasion at Capistrano Beach in California, a game of cards started in the living room around 9.00 in the evening. By 11.00 he was in trouble but Daley would not let go. No one was allowed to go home until he won. He woke me up as excited as if he'd won the Olympic gold, to tell me he had done so at 2.00am!

And there are, of course, other arenas where winners can find themselves, but not of their own volition. For sure they are not a frequent occurrence, but they can happen. In these situations, their attitude and almost intuitive response is that uncertainty is simply a given in life and they seek to turn uncertainty to personal and collective advantage. If assistance is required to do so, they know where to access and recruit it, or they find someone who can; they own responsibility for making that assistance work for them mentally, emotionally and physically.

They see winning as a never ending story, that there is always a sense of achievement, yet there is always another step to go. There is no sense of having finally arrived. There is always someone to be bettered: themselves. There is always another, tougher mountain to climb because they know that it's only by scaling these mountains they will make 'better' happen.

They are strong on personal values and standards and believe, like Don Shula, *'if you don't stand for something, you fall for anything'*. They are people who get things done. They are action people who would rather take a hit for doing something than for doing nothing. They know that failure is not about the result going against them, but about walking away or not trying. Failures, to them, are people who blame others, never themselves.

The Risk of Winning

So winners live on the edge. Winners take the risk of winning because they know there is no such thing as risk in losing. Anyone can do that so where's the risk? Daley Thompson summed this up when I asked him at the Rome 1987 World Championships if he was sure he could perform the way he needed to while carrying an injury. 'If you never try, you never know' was his response. Those who really understand how tough it is to get through the ten events of decathlon, even without injury, remember his courage and character in seeing it through to finishing out of the medals – as one of the greatest performances of a great winner. Winners, then, are aware that they have their time in their arenas and have their own energy to deal with the challenges they face. No one else has that time and energy. Winners use every moment and every drop of energy to be who they must be; to make a better life for those whom they touch and influence with their time and energy.

I am sure this concept is what Oliver Wendell Holmes had in mind when writing:

> *'Many people die with their music still in them. Why is this so? Too often it is because they are always getting ready to live. Before they know it, time runs out'.*[6]

Wayne Bennett who coached Brisbane Broncos Rugby League team and is, in my opinion, one of the greatest coaches of any sport, underlined this in his book 'Don't Die With the Music in You'.[7]

I believe you are a winner or you would not have picked up 'Winning Matters'. It is your choice to find out just how great a winner you are and can be in today's arenas and in all the tougher ones to follow. That greatness is your music. Only you can play your music. So let's hear it.

Chapter 2

CHANGE TO WIN

Change is like a game. We are in that game every minute of our lives and we can become its victims and be defeated by it; or we can go for the win. The choice is ours to have a winning attitude. The game may be at the cultural dimension or the moment by moment dimension of the arena now. Whether trying to lead change or being led through change, the objective remains as constant as change itself: to win and to keep on winning.

Be Comfortable with Change

We all accept the simple basic truism that change is constant. We acknowledge as George Bernard Shaw[1] stated, *'those who cannot change their minds, cannot change anything'*. We agree that the journey to achieving our goals is seldom a straight line affair. Rather, it is a continuous process of adjusting, adapting and redirecting to get there. That is the case whatever the nature or theatre of change. It can be in how we conduct business or deal with personal economics as a consequence of the pretty devastating changes in the winter of 2008/09, or it can be how the regularly amended rules, regulations and laws in our competitive arenas oblige us to examine the relevance of our established skills; what new skills and competencies we must learn; and how we apply

19

Culture does not change because we desire to change it. Culture changes when the organisation is transformed; the culture reflects the realities of people working together every day.

Frances Hesselbein[2]

People don't resist change, they resist being changed.

Peter Senge[3]

You must take personal responsibility. You cannot change the circumstances, the seasons, or the wind, but you can change yourself.

Jim Rohn[4]

them personally and collectively under pressure. That pressure is due to the accelerating speed of change; to the uncertainty and unpredictability of change; to its complexity and diversity; and to an ambiguity in the value it brings against what its cost may be.

We know all of this, but will we all persistently live it? Probably not, because most people would prefer to change only when they feel like it or when they have to and, hopefully, that's not too often! The fact is, even for those who would claim to be committed to it, changing what we do, what works for us now, or the way we have always done things around here brings at least uneasy adoption, or at worst, distress or rejection.

Wherever we are in that range of response is probably something to do with discomfort, uncertainty, disorientation, even fear. After all, it is hard to change technically or, even more so, behaviourally and there may be some reluctance to do so and resentment of those putting that challenge to us. It is important to recognise that this is the case before we embark on a campaign of creating a culture which embraces and leverages change to advantage. This is because everyone in our organisation and our enterprise, ourselves included, will be impacted by change in terms of what they do and how they do it. By impact, I mean physically, mentally and emotionally.

A Change Culture

So how can we effectively, and with the least possible pain to our people, approach the task and deliver the changes, so that we become intuitive in being adaptable when change is happening to us and creative when we are making change happen? I believe that for real change to happen, there are three dimensions which must be addressed simultaneously. In doing so, progress in each contributes to making progress towards achieving the outcomes we need in the others.

There is the macro dimension which relates to overall culture change and strategic levels. This represents *what we can become*. Next there is the meso dimension which relates to competition campaigns such as world class performance plans, business plans, sports seasons, Olympiads, business years and so on. This represents *what we must consistently be*. Finally we have the micro dimension which relates to what we must deliver fairly, squarely, decently and by the rules at any moment in our arena; day after day; match by match; week by week. This represents *what we persistently do*.

The use of macro, meso and micro dimension terminology is to emphasize that there is a symbiosis or interdependence here. I believe that what players do and how they do it successfully in the arena (micro) reflects the overall culture and strategy (macro) which, in turn, shapes concept design and delivery of the year/campaign plan (meso).

So, for coach Ric Charlesworth creating versatility and flexibility in the Australian Women's Hockey Team 'The Hockeyroos' which culminated in back to back Olympic Gold in Atlanta (1996) and Sydney (2000) reflected a changing Australian coaching and performance culture started in the early 1980s.

Peter Keen virtually reinvented UK Cycling culture and changed the discipline of year plans within their world class performance plan in the late 1980s and early 1990s. David Brailsford built on that and created an attitude to constantly delivering agility in adapting to and responding to changing standards and competitive challenges in the arena. This was achieved by absorbing quickly, then effectively applying within the cyclists' preparation programmes, the rapid expansion of sports technology, sports sciences and training theory.

It is most often the case that we have no idea why our organisation's culture is the way it is. We believe in it simply because 'that's the way things happen around here!' And those who created the prevailing culture are probably no longer involved. We normally just accept it as an inherited tradition, if not ritual. I mean, it clearly works for us, so why challenge the accepted order of things?

Now please don't get me wrong, I am not saying that everything in culture is wrong in terms of what people do and how they do it. It is just that there should be a mindset where we regularly challenge each action to see if our performances and results can be better when done differently or when we do different things. I want that mindset to be applied whether it is in how we run our sport or business; or how we win our games and achieve our business targets.

You see, change is not a once and for all thing we do today and that is it. It is a never ending journey and commitment to involvement in that journey. It is an essential part of the culture we need to win time and time again in today's and tomorrow's competitive arenas. Change, then, is a continuous process not a product.

Owning Change

So it does not need a crisis or a new broom to decide it's time for review and change. Our cultures, campaign plans and game plans should be constantly reviewed and changed because that is the way we do things around here! I believe that the changing world we are in and the curiosity and imagination we all have can initiate a change process in the blink of an eye. Sometimes the opportunity can be there, yet we don't see it because we see what it is in the context of what we have done up till now, not what it could mean to make us change how we will do things. For example, until the 1960s, to be a successful high jumper in track and field, your technique had to meet three conditions:

- Jump as high as possible off one leg
- Avoid dislodging the bar
- Land safely

The third condition was important because landing areas were pretty hazardous affairs!

So coaches, helped by experts in biomechanics, had concluded that the most effective technique was the 'straddle' where athletes 'belly rolled' around and faced the bar to land on their sides. This became accepted convention in the culture of high jumping. It was how the business of high jump was conducted and prepared for. Everyone did it. As the 1960s unwound, aware of the need for greater safety and comfort, landing areas were improved from being at ground level to being raised mounds of sawdust and rubber chippings, to a giant, thick, soft, foam-rubber mattress. The world culture of high jump rejoiced at this change. From strategy; to year plan, to technical execution, people saw that you could continue to do things the way you always did, but now you'd be more comfortable doing it. Everyone in the world agreed.

Everyone, that is, except a young student from Medford, Oregon, USA who could not do 'straddle'. He saw the change differently. He focused only on the first two conditions. You did not have to do 'straddle' if it didn't matter how you landed. You could probably land on the giant mattress on your head and still live to tell the tale! So, he invented his own technique, going over the bar on his back. In 1968 he won the Olympic Gold Medal in Mexico City; the only athlete in the world using that technique. The culture argued about it and some parts of the culture outlawed it! Today, every high jumper in the world uses the 'Fosbury Flop' technique developed by Dick Fosbury, because he saw opportunity in change, then chose to challenge the accepted order.

People Changing People

Once we accept the need for a culture and people that live change, how do we move things on to make it happen? If there is a key to being successful in this, it is to ensure we avoid the perception that we are imposing change. That perception cannot be allowed to get a foothold, whether with the people on the receiving end or with those who are the leaders and directors of change. When imposition is the perception, the central issue is not lack of ability to change, but lack of will. In such a climate, people hear what they most fear, and such trauma has a lengthy shelf life!

Let me explain. Conventional culture looks like this *(figure 2)*. It has a hierarchical shape from board members to work teams. Even if the organisation has different titles, this is its shape. At every level there is a range of person from enthusiast to cynic. To the left of enthusiasts there are nut cases, to the right of cynics there are terrorists! Hopefully, you don't have these extremes in your organisations. We know this is the case, but cultures which pursue conventional change do it this way *(figure 3)*. The board agree to the change and pass it to senior management who know better so they compromise it! They pass to

Figure 2

Conventional Culture

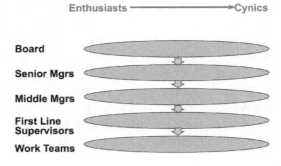

Figure 3

Conventional Culture Change

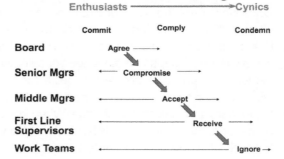

Figure 4

Real Culture Change

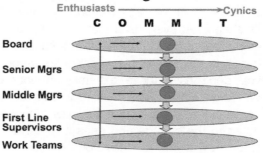

middle management who accept it. Front line managers receive it. Work teams then ignore it! It's just another flavour of the month – a sheep dip. We all know how to deal with these babies. We just keep our heads down, stand up again when the coast is clear and then do what we always did!

Moreover, because it is perceived that change is being imposed from the top, an 'us' and 'them' situation occurs, with three populations emerging as a consequence. There are those who commit to the change; those who comply with it, and those who condemn it.

The most dangerous people here are not those who condemn. In fact, they are quite useful in that you can rely on them to spot problem areas! Provided they are not actively and aggressively preventing progress, they should be treated like a river treats a rock: just go round them! Be aware, however, of what they say and do, so that you can make effective responses. No, the problem people are those who comply. They disguise themselves, pretending to be on-side, but they are actually 'wait and see' people who are not punching their weight to make change happen. Because they disguise their attitude with smiles and nods, they are tough to identify. And because they are not really pulling their weight to make change happen, progress is being compromised.

So we have to take a different approach to leading change *(figure 4)*. We support and leverage the buy-in and a sense of change ownership in those committed at all levels. Through them we can work to build support in converting the compliers and maybe even those who condemn. At each level throughout the organisation we build a critical mass of change champions who are, and create, a team of 'change coaches'. At a stroke, we make the drive for the changes we seek, from attitude to behaviour to action, the responsibility of everyone

The most successful person is the one who holds onto the old just as long as it is good, and grabs the new just as soon as it is better.

Robert P. Vanderpoel[5]

To live is to change, and to be perfect is to change often.

John Henry, Cardinal Newman[6]

Your success in life isn't based on your ability to simply change. It's based on your ability to change faster than your competition, customers and business.

Mark Sanborn[7]

at every level from policy maker to player. We are each accountable.

The double headed vertical arrow is for the two critical qualities of leadership and creativity we rely on to fuel this approach to leading change at every level. First, some think that leadership comes from the top. Of course, the style of leadership does. However, once we have coached our people to take personal ownership in changing things for the better; and to take others with them to make it happen, everyone at every level can be a leader when required to be so. So, we coach all our people to develop and exercise their leadership qualities.

Next, some think that creativity as a quality is only the domain of those who understand what life is like in the front line. How can those further from it be creative at such a distance? The fact is, every two-year old demonstrates extraordinary creativity given something as simple as a large cardboard box. It can be a tardis, spaceship, submarine or castle – anything their young imaginations wish it to be. We have all been two-year olds at least once in our lives, so creativity is there within all of us! We must coach our people to develop and exercise their own creativity whether they are the work teams or the board.

We effect the change then, by coaching creative leadership throughout the organisation. This means our leaders must work towards change driven by the hopes and aspirations of all those who are not only effected by, but who will deliver the change. Their ownership of this process will mean that change is pursued because it is desired rather than demanded, and such change will always be more enduring. Ownership here is about hearts as well as heads.

Hard though it may be, we must work as a leadership team to transform the perception of change as a revolutionary process to an evolutionary one. Remember, the culture you are building towards; your strategy and planning and the way you compete in the arena, become the energy that makes positive change happen. It is for us, in our very DNA, to persistently seek and act effectively on every opportunity to do so.

Managing the Process

From the start and in every step of the journey, it is essential to build and constantly reinforce trust in the process of change and those leading it at whatever level. This means establishing a sense of genuine involvement through being listened to and being kept in the picture. Quality regular communication, then, in all its forms, is paramount. Best endeavours on everyone's part will seldom be enough to ensure full buy-in at every level. So in working to effect change of attitude and perception, our leadership must be competent not only to make such change happen, but to manage problems arising from existing attitudes and perceptions. If these problems are not addressed we will fail to change attitude and perception. We will also seriously compromise pursuit of our overall objective and put achieving it in doubt.

Managing Attitudes and Perceptions

Leadership must raise energies to create solutions and encourage involvement whilst simultaneously managing the negatives.

Leadership must

- Gather and communicate all relevant intelligence

regularly. Where information is 'classified', explain why.

- Establish and exercise a coaching culture, not only for the change process but as a central feature in supporting continuous learning.

- Recruit strong honest partners and champions.

- Keep any stress that people might experience at a productive level.

- Create a conduit where opinions on issues can be expressed and demonstrate that they are noted and considered.

- Identify opposition; keep them close; and be vigilant for hidden agendas.

- Develop the personal mindset of being able to view events both as an actor on stage experiencing the action, and as director on the balcony leading it.

Raise energies to

- Increase light:

  - To pay attention to real issues and challenges.

  - To focus attention on hard issues so that they bring conflicts into the open.

  - To accept responsibility for tackling and solving these issues.

- Reduce heat:

  - To avoid turmoil.

  - To focus on specific technical challenges *(what we do)*.

  - To address behavioural challenges *(how we do things)*.

Create solutions

- Create a climate for providing solutions to make progress:

  - Establish focus groups on specific issues/matters.

  - Establish operational rules based on agreed values.

  - Set time-scales.

  - Establish reporting relationships.

  - Keep it 'human' *(this is about people!)*.

  - Recognise both hopes and fears for the future.

Encourage involvement

- Place tasks, actions and delivery where they belong. This is not only the key to making necessary change it is actually the objective we are aiming for within the culture, the business/world class performance plan, or the game plan in the arena today:

  - Don't provide solutions/answers; provide challenges to generate desire **to** change and **for** change.

  - Transfer ownership of problem solving to others.

  - Have everyone accept personally that they must address the challenge of adaptation to change and of being creative in making change happen.

Manage the negatives

As the process of change gains momentum, leadership may be exposed to one of several experiences.

- Direct attack – this can even be personal on character and style.

- Side tracked – being undermined in taking the overall process forward by being obliged to focus on a single issue.

- Seduced by fans – being distracted by the intensity of that relationship, from demanding necessary changes in them.

- Diverted by fire fighting – getting confused between what is important and what is urgent.

We must be prepared to cope with such situations on a daily basis, by aligning what we do between agreed values and the vision we are working to realise. Leadership must also be alert to possible experiences of those who are the focus of the change process.

- Irritation at being moved from comfort zone of normal routine.

- Sense of loss of what they had *(and sometimes loss of colleagues).*

- Weakening of self esteem/belief.

- Disillusionment.

- Stress of re-orientation.

- Questioning competence and loyalty of organisation.

- Fear.

If any of these have been allowed to grow, we must again review how effective we have been in managing attitudes and perceptions. Once spotted, and review conducted, personal coaching should be immediately available for the persons exposed to such experience, and continued until they become a productive contributor to success of the process. More often than not, this is mostly about building trust and sense of involvement through better communications.

No matter how good we believe our communication system to be in our organisation, it must be persistently reviewed and improved. Communication must be a constant and consistent part of daily life from strategic design through development to delivery. It is the lifeblood of the organisation, especially in making change happen.

In the moment by moment action of the arena, coaches advise players to talk to each other. This is as much about reinforcement of trust and confidence throughout the team as it is to motivate and pass on technical support to help colleagues perform better. Such advice applies throughout an entire organisation and whatever the dimension of change you can make it happen in your arena.

Chapter 3

LEADING EDGE

We are all leaders the moment we take ownership of a situation and take people with us in turning it to advantage. As ownership is a critical focus in coaching our people and ourselves, we must develop the leadership skills we have. For some, that development will take them on a career journey shaped by personal style and which may lead to senior leadership roles.

Leadership Difference

I believe that we all have leadership skills, but we don't all choose to develop and use them. In a culture committed to winning, we must. In that winning culture, people take ownership of turning each moment to advantage for the organisation. As this invariably means taking people with you to achieve the necessary advantage, you need the ability to effectively exercise those skills.

So what does a leader do? The most succinct explanation is attributed to Henry Kissinger.[1]

> *'The task of a leader is to get his people from where they are to where they have not been.'*

The leader

- **Seeks the moment** to make a winning difference for the team.

- **Seizes the moment** by making the right decision on what to do in taking people with them to make it happen.

- **Never doubts for a moment** that together they will make a winning difference. They imbue in everyone that belief.

People you lead today may tomorrow lead in owning a moment of opportunity and taking you with them in turning it to advantage. So, leadership is not about creating followership, it's about creating ownership. The leader ensures that the people led are well prepared to take ownership of their role in an endeavour; just as the leader must be prepared for his or hers. Ownership means just what it says. People must be given freedom to exercise ownership and accept the responsibility and accountability that go with it.

In a culture where everyone has developed and delivers leadership skills, some will have both drive and ability to grow towards senior leadership roles in an organisation. They are the people who will ultimately be chief executives, head coaches, presidents, captains, team managers or some equivalent role. It seems to me that a culture becomes a powerful achievement generator when everyone lives the idea of delivering personal ownership of applying leadership skills. This is described by Peter Senge[2] as:

> 'The passion at the heart of every human undertaking comes from the deep longing of

human beings to make a difference; to have
an impact. It comes from giving rather than
taking, and being appreciated for that.'

The leader is the winning difference and is both the architect and the face of change. In a team where all are prepared to lead, to make a difference, to make change happen, the great leader wants to be the leader of leaders and has ambition to do so. As a leader, you know that the basic drive to be better and different lies in everyone. You know you do not have to create it. It is there already. So you re-energise it and work for your people to maintain and grow it. Some will then go on, like you, to make leadership a career. All will get more out of themselves, because you have cultivated a climate where people's passion can be safely articulated.

The great leader's drive is relentless to realise his or her professional life dreams. To get there, you know you must create a shared sense of purpose which has meaning and significance for the people you lead. They need that sense of shared purpose if they are to operate as a team of involved, committed people. So leadership is about building teamship on a platform of ownership. It must, of course, be anchored in realities, so vision and values become the rudder and compass for decision making throughout their purposeful journey to the dream.

The entrepreneur may not in the early stages of an enterprise have great need of leadership skills. They are driving their own dream and so anyone brought in initially to help make the dream happen must fit exactly into the role and performance expectations of the entrepreneur. However, there comes a critical point in the growth of the business when leadership skills become essential. Such skills must be developed or growth is compromised. Our people must share the dream and be developed for, involved in and committed to realising it. The entrepreneur must never lose his or her sense of drive and vision, but must now take on board leadership qualities which generate the will for development, involvement and commitment in their people. John Viney[3] is right to say that *it is imagination which fuels the entrepreneur'* and the people are the engine which realises the vision.

Critical Focus

A leader takes people where they want to go. A great leader takes people where they need to go, even when they don't want to. In this, you not only need technical expertise but people expertise. This means having the character to impose and the personality to impress. In team situations, although there is complexity in all of this, when handling powerful egos and personal differences in delivering cohesion, the leader will understand what is going out of focus, then quickly and effectively re-adjust.

In the season following Michael Jordon's retirement from the Chicago Bulls, they made the NBA Eastern Conference Finals. In a best of seven games series, they trailed New York Nicks 2-0 and in the third game the score was tied at 117-117. Phil Jackson, the Bulls coach called a time out with four seconds remaining. Scottie Pippin had become Bulls top player but was certainly not a Michael Jordan. Jackson had had to restructure how the Bulls played as things could not now be so pivotal on the genius of one player. Jackson called for Pippin to take the throw in to Tony Kukoc who would take the shot. As the players walked on to the court, Jackson saw Pippin sitting on the bench and asked him if he was in or out. 'Out' replied Pippin. Jackson then instructed Pete Myers to throw in to Kukoc. The game recommenced.

Kukoc scored. The Bulls won.

There was elation as the team headed for the changing room but there was also a dark cloud for what some perceived as insubordination or petulance at not being given the chance to shoot the winning points. It was a situation which no responsible leader could let pass without comment. Different leaders would probably offer quite different solutions as to how the situation might be handled, and several could be effective. I really like Jackson's. Bearing in mind the need to grow a different sense of team dynamics, Jackson stood at the changing room door until all had entered. Then, he said 'what happened out there hurt us. This is your team. It's for you to sort it out.' He closed the door and left them to do just that.

This is pretty impressive and courageous leadership and underlines the tough reality and real value of giving ownership in a team context. If Jackson had confronted Pippin, the issue would have become one that involved only the two of them. It was a team issue, it had to involve the team. All had to understand their personal responsibility in making the team what it must be.

A Matter of Style

Students of leadership styles suggest that there are several. Not all research agrees on how many. Most agree that it is 'important' to be able to fit style to situation. The fact is that leaders reach senior positions because their strengths have worked well enough to get them there. It is as much about their character and personality as their abilities. It is about who they are. So these very strengths have been constantly reinforced on the journey and it is unlikely that they will be abandoned. The leaders have learned to play the hand they have been dealt. They make

*My own definition of leadership is this:
the capacity and the will to rally men and
women to a common purpose and the
character which inspires confidence.*

General Montgomery[4]

*The task of leadership is not to
put greatness into humanity,
but to elicit it, for the
greatness is already there.*

John Buchan[5]

*Our chief want is someone who will inspire
us to be what we know we could be.*

Ralph Waldo Emerson[6]

it their winning hand. Of course they learn, make adjustments and take things on board over time. They may also accept personal coaching to deal with rough edges or things that reduce their effectiveness. In essence they are who they are and that has profound impact on their style. This must be shaped and polished, not scrapped simply because it doesn't fit with some imagined model of leadership perfection. So, your leadership style is, in many ways, how you have lived the story of your life. That means no two leaders will lead in exactly the same way. Be world class with your way by persistently working on making it even better!

In both sport and business each type of leader may achieve great things but from quite different positions of strength. The main types I would suggest are as follows, although you will come across a few hybrids!

Top of the Class
These leaders are bright, intellectual heavyweights in their field. They attract admiring disciples, but they are only effective as leaders if their high IQ is matched by high emotional intelligence. This type of leader will be found at the head of organisations where there are very high academic demands.

Dictators
These leaders are the controlling autocrat type. They accept only their very high personal standards of excellence and sub-consciously feel no one else is at their level. They are a huge asset when goals must be achieved in short time scales and in crisis situations.

Monarch of the Glen
These leaders are the archetypal leaders of long established businesses and especially family businesses.

They reached their position often as a right of succession. They bring a sense of reliability and stability in traditional cultures. People feel safe with them as the caring champions of the culture. They enrich traditions of enduring quality.

The Natural
These leaders feel at home in the position and look that way to colleagues and team makers. They are almost intuitive in calling the right shots whatever the situation. They are 'the man for all seasons'.

Commander
These leaders are like military commanders – very high in strategic design within a framework of accepted discipline. They lead their teams through tough campaigns. They will be supported by strong generals as strategy deliverers. Whilst in the arena, their team's reputation rightly grows as persistent campaign victors. On the one hand this frightens the opposition; on the other it builds immense belief in the leader throughout the team.

Cat Herder
These leaders nudge and prod team members to take the direction the leader intends them to. They are known as people who understand people, especially their people. They are perceived as caring leaders. They appreciate that egos and ambitions can take people off the track of common purpose, but they are firm in redirecting them. Organisations that see change as evolution rather than revolution need them.

Charismatic
These leaders are people magnets. They have a DNA advantage in that people instinctively go with them. Charisma on its own, however, is only a short term

advantage and can too easily, if unconsciously, be abused to conceal absence of real leadership quality.

Leaders, over time, must recognise where their type and style of leadership holds advantage or disadvantage. As suggested above, no one can change who they are. So, the really great leaders build a leadership team around them to provide those strengths of type and style which they personally lack. They then guide the very real strength that their leadership team represents in applying that collective range of competencies to the kaleidoscopic diversity of actions, behaviours and relationships their people represent. It is about understanding compensation.

Ion Tiriac, the internationally acclaimed entrepreneur who managed Boris Becker, once told me that all great tennis players play the way they do because they uniquely manage their own technical compensations. They need to create their own personal style as a strength. No player enjoys perfect scores in all aspects of the game so they must compensate. That also applies to great leaders. No one would score ten out of ten in all the qualities they need access to but they excellently manage the compensations.

Leading Characteristics

There are enough books to fill a library on the subject of competencies and qualities essential to a leader, so it would be pointless to list such here. However, I have been really fortunate both in sport and in business, to meet and work with some truly great leaders. All demonstrated the following characteristics in some measure. Not all have demonstrated the same characteristics in the same measure. Nevertheless, these leaders are extremely successful, so I thought it might be useful to go through these characteristics here.

Vision
They dream big. There is a restlessness to their imagination because they constantly generate a churn of ideas they know they will realise through their people. The greatest are true visionaries.

Respect
They value respect above affection. They respect the value of everyone in the organisation, whatever their role.

Restless
They are uncomfortable at feeling comfortable. It is a bit like the Formula 1 driver Mario Andretti's line *'if you feel in control you aren't going fast enough'*. There is never a feeling of having arrived. Peter Godfrey of American Express Global Network Services, created a program for his leadership team entitled 'Who Dares Leads' with the object of being effective when leadership is tested in extreme situations. This, he believes will be the differentiator in leadership excellence in the toughest business arenas. He's right.

Heat Seeking
There is always a next step to be taken where they will challenge themselves to do something different and always to be better. They are climbing the next mountain in their mind before they have reached the summit of this one. They endeavour to have everyone in the team think the same way. They go to where the action is hottest. In the words of Steve Kerr a former American basketball player, *'if you are not taking flak, you're not over the target.'*

Standards

They set very high standards for themselves and expect this to be instinctive in their people. These standards apply both to what is done and how it is done, so they are unequivocally and strongly values based. For example the late Anita Roddick ensured that none of the products sold in the Body Shop involved testing on animals.

Strategic

They are benchmarks of excellence in their preparation of design in strategy; in creating the design itself; and in driving its delivery. They are meticulous in attention to even the smallest detail. Dave Tanner and Jurgen Groebler in British Rowing, not only transformed their own sport in this respect to deliver outstanding achievement at Olympic Games and World Championships, but also changed mindsets of Olympic sports in general.

Agile

Although almost ruthlessly focussed on vision and strategy delivery, they are extraordinarily agile to the point of being reflexive in responding where they see change and adjustment will give advantage. Ric Charlesworth in Australian women's hockey and Luis Aragonis in Spanish football based player development on the probability that strategy delivery would require constant change and adjustment. To embrace the advantage laser eye surgery would bring to the already successful business of his Optical Express brand, David Moulsdale pioneered the changing perception of vision care in Europe.

Knowledge Hungry

They are hungry to learn by listening, watching and experiencing and will search for knowledge as much from sources outside their own speciality arena as in it.

Great leaders are almost always great simplifiers, who can cut through argument, debate and doubt to offer a solution everybody can understand.

General Colin Powell[7]

Management is efficiency in climbing the ladder of success; leadership determines whether the ladder is leaning against the right wall.

Stephen R. Covey[8]

Leadership is intentional influence.

Michael McKinney[9]

Philanthropist, Tom Hunter, created the Entrepreneurial Exchange so that entrepreneurs might learn from each other and the diverse arenas in which they competed.

Communication

They are excellent, clear communicators who know exactly how to get their message through. Whether it is in making people aware of hard facts in unambiguous language or persuading people to go with an idea through metaphor, there is always a flavour of inspiration that underpins the message. Shakespeare ensured that heroic leaders were afforded this quality in his plays. Many great sport, business and political leaders have and do set themselves apart in the power of their oratory to the point where having studied the best, they work at it until their own is a work of art.

Focused

All are intuitive in differentiating between what will interfere with progress and what will not. After the 1964 Tokyo Olympic Games, an exhibition challenge was arranged in Warsaw, where the Polish head coach in fencing fought Poland's Olympic gold medalists. The coach beat them all. When asked afterwards how this could be, he replied 'I have learned to identify the wrong cues faster than them'. This is about learning to read the game and responding only to the bits that matter. The greatest educator here, is experience.

Resilient

They are resilient and persistent whether the challenge is from the opposition or from changes in conditions and circumstances. In every arena there is always the possibility of being thrown off balance, so great leaders practice how they will use that moment not only to achieve better balance, but to knock the opponent off balance in the process. There's a lot to be learned from martial arts in terms of the principles involved here.

Radar
They establish excellent personal radar. There are some areas of intelligence that colleagues share but are disinclined to do so when a person is appointed or promoted to a leadership position. The person is no longer one of the gang! The leader must, then, create his or her own radar to ensure all relevant intelligence reaches him or her. That means accessing the painful bad news stuff as well as the good. They will develop a filter in this radar that gets rid of the worthless stuff. So they enjoy the great line by Hank Ketcham, creator of Dennis the Menace cartoon strip, *'flattery in life is like chewing gum. Enjoy it but don't swallow it.'*

Microscope
They must also be aware of always being under the microscope. Once in a leadership role, the leader is being watched and listened to constantly. What is seen and heard must be what the leader needs to be perceived. There can be no ambiguity. Henry II, King of England, was unhappy at the persistence of Thomas à Becket, an advisor he appointed as Archbishop of Canterbury, in telling him things he did not want to hear. The king reportedly commented 'Who will rid me of this truculent priest?' Four leading knights of court took this to mean - who will kill him for me? So, in 1170 they murdered Thomas à Becket in Canterbury Cathedral. That may not have been the king's intention! Be sure that perceptions are what you intend them to be because perception is reality for most people.

Spark Gap
They are sensitive in managing the spark gap. I think there is a very critical space that separates a leader from

a member of the team. It's like the gap in a spark plug. The gap is so small it can hardly be seen by the naked eye. So why have the gap? Why not get rid of it?

As a young teacher just out of college, I worked at Worksop College, a boarding school. I remember enjoying coffee on Sunday evenings with some final year students who I was coaching in athletics. After all, they were only a few years younger than me! The headmaster took me to one side. 'Don't get too close or they won't understand who you are. The boys are the boys, the staff are the staff. They must see space between the two.'

If the gap is closed there is no spark. So why not make the gap really wide so that there is no doubt that it is there? If the gap is too wide again there is no spark.

Every leader understands that there must be just the right space to make the spark happen. Only you will know what your spark gap must be. And whatever it is for you, it must be managed well.

Courage

They do whatever it takes, even the unimaginable, to effect necessary change. After the Hungarian uprising in 1956, the brilliant Hungarian Football team broke up. The captain, Ferenc Puskas, went to Spain and joined Real Madrid in 1958. He was one of the top goal scorers in international football and already, Real Madrid had Alfredo Di Stéfano – the highest goal scorer in the Spanish league.

A lot of weight is attached to the title of top goal scorer in Spain. In their first season together Puskas and Di Stéfano were soon rivals for the top spot. The rivalry was so strong that the changing room was beginning to divide into those who would set up the scoring opportunity for one rather than the other. This created a non-cohesive team on the field and consequently the performance was short of where it could be.

In the last game of the season each had the same number of goals for the season. Late in the game Puskas masterfully cut through the opposition defence and had only the goal keeper to beat when he spotted Di Stéfano unmarked. He passed the ball to Di Stéfano, who scored and finished the season as Spain's top goal scorer. That pass changed the team's perception of how they must play to be as great as they could be. Some would see that as the defining moment which launched an era of outstanding achievement of Real Madrid. I see it as a piece of leadership genius.

Decisions

Finally, and above all else, their capacity to make the right decisions even under the most intense pressure separates the great leader from the average. Moreover, they have an ingrained sense of accountability which ensures they never walk away from responsibility for that decision nor its consequence. They know and have humility when it goes right (which is most of the time) and acknowledge the value of their team in that outcome. They know when it didn't and hold their hand up for the mistake. And, whatever the outcome, they enjoy an excitement in anticipating the next moment of decision.

Learning the leadership Ropes

Because decision making is at the crux of so much in 'Winning Matters', it is covered in more detail in Chapter 4. The drive and ability which triggers the decision to make leadership a career choice does not guarantee a senior leadership position nor leadership greatness but they are certainly prerequisites! How far someone goes in their leadership journey has to be actively worked for. It is in taking personal responsibility for continuous learning through the experience of that journey, that the characteristics discussed here, liberally spiced with the tips for coaches in Chapter 8 and whatever advice is extracted from all the leadership books out there, prepares an aspiring leader to go all the way to the top.

I think the journey has two dimensions to it. The first is what's learned in going through the hierarchy of competencies associated with different levels of role in an organisation. The second is the stage by stage development structure for the aspiring leader.

Role Progression

In the first dimension, each level of role is associated with certain competencies.

Performer
This is when you start working for an organisation. There is an element of selection at this point – both by the organisation in seeking the best person for the job; and by the individual in choosing this organisation to work for. At this point, you have not only been identified as having talent, skills, knowledge, work ethic and desire to learn, but you are acutely aware of that yourself, and are out to prove you are a top performer.

Team Member
Next you become a valued and effective team member. You contribute to the team in pursuit of the team's common purpose by constantly delivering role excellence,

and are effective in connecting, complementing and communicating with team members in the dynamics that make for a cohesive team unit. This is where concepts of interdependence and balance are learned and applied.

Manager
The next step is the role of manager. Here, you organise people and the resources required to achieve team goals. In this, a key skill is to make the complex simple in getting things done and giving an order to that process.

Leader
Now, comes the effective leader position. You win your people's commitment to achieving the organisation's vision by living its values. You are the catalyst for making necessary change happen through your people. You set the standards that define excellence in living the organisation's values.

Senior Leader
Finally, you are in the most senior leadership territory. It is the goal of those aspiring leaders who want to go the distance to get there. This is a person who builds enduring greatness for the organisation. The greatest are a paradox in that they exercise what appear to be conflicting attributes selectively when one or the other is demanded to create or cope with a situation. So, there can be humility or overpowering self belief: modesty or wilfulness; the velvet touch or the iron fist. The shift from one to the other can be as fast as a chameleon changing colour.

Of course, it could be a mistake to think that senior leadership territory is only about the competencies suggested here. Rather they are the cumulative translation and absorption of those competencies learned through the experience of all the roles in the journey, in some shape or form. From workplace to senior leadership opportunity, each role affords a practical workshop for all the competencies and lessons that you may need to call upon to establish the brand and quality of leadership that will be uniquely yours.

The Career Journey

The second dimension commences the moment someone decides leadership is for them. So, in terms of the player to senior leadership journey, it will certainly have been an intention by the time someone is into management. Often, it is even before the person has become a player. These would be my coaching tips to anyone who decides to go the whole distance not simply to being a senior leader, but a great one. My tips relate to seven stages of the journey.

The Acceptor or Embryonic Leader

The moment you decide you want to be a leader, you must identify role models, heroes or those whose leadership wisdom you respect, then recruit from them a mentor or mentors. In fact, it is from this moment that you operate a personal discipline in creating the right mentor network as you progress through each stage of the journey.

When I decided that coaching would be my career, I was like some kind of 'stalker' following around the best athletics coaches of the time at major championships. I'd watch everything they did in training grounds and listen to their coaching comments. I'd even eavesdrop on their conversation to find out where they would be going for a beer in the evenings so that I could listen in! I suppose I was a real pain the neck, but it was a great university for me! The right mentors at this stage set you in the right direction. They change how you will live your life.

The Explorer or Apprentice Leader

Once given early opportunity in a management or junior leadership role, it is time to try and use the theory of books, lectures and courses in the real world! Normally, this is a low key entry into leadership. Best advice here is to serve what amounts to an accountable apprenticeship alongside a battle-hardened veteran of many campaigns. It is a bit like a newly graduated young officer learning what life is really all about under the watchful eye of a tough sergeant major: tough he or she will be; builder of a career foundation he or she is; protect you from harm he or she will. There should also be the continued input from a mentor who can help relate what is learned here to the overall journey.

The Challenger or Emergent Leader

Now comes the moment when you are appointed to a leadership role where, for the first time, you feel like you are flying solo. Often, this is a promotion above your peers and team-mates. This is where the 'spark-gap' must be clearly understood and applied. You must set and tune boundaries and relationships. There are still many questions to be asked in what to do and how to do it as part of self managed learning in growing as a leader, so selected confidants are essential mentors. These will be drawn from established senior leaders in their own field and, of special value here, from leaders who have only one or two years experience more than you.

You must learn to prioritise, when to build momentum, how to hold the ship steady and when to fire-fight. Mistakes will be made in taking considered risks, even when all the homework has been done, as you explore new ground. Mistakes are an essential part of the growing process and are OK provided you remember three things that must be done with them:

- Own up to them
- Learn from them
- Don't repeat them

Your mentors must be trusted to guide you through the learning process and help you avoid repetition. And they can only do that if you admit the mistake. Some tough stuff, like dismissing people, brings an awareness that the emotional lives of your people are in your hands. Mentors will be key to developing the necessary emotional intelligence for this.

The Winner or Breakthrough Leader

Growing confidence through cumulative experience takes you closer to a more senior leadership level. The art of leadership grows out of its science. An information network is vital to refining the art whilst never losing the sharpness of understanding the synthesis input from the performance and leadership sciences. It is also time to bring in people who will challenge your strengths and compensate where you are vulnerable. You learn to lead a leadership team. You nurture those whose star shines brightly and know that, in turn, they make yours shine brighter.

This is where it is increasingly important to identify and access those people from a range of disciplines, to broaden the leadership mindset and to bring new perspective to making the big decisions. Normally, in the previous stages, you will have looked for mentors or advisors who are senior, older and more experienced people in general. Now, things change as you also look to younger people whose specific expertise, energy and creativity complement the wisdom of the more experienced. This introduces a 'why not' attitude not only to your approach, but to the culture of the organisation.

The Champion or Peak Performance Leader
Now come the peak performance years where you are at your most productive and effective in delivering your senior leadership role. Strength of confidants, alliances and networks are built. 'Radar and microscope' are very strictly applied as you persistently listen for the truth. You heed warnings and listen even to the jokes that persist, to check for serious messages. Not all rumours are rubbish!

It is as if the radar has become as essential to your continued functioning effectiveness as the immune system is to your body. You become master of transparency and openness in bringing values consistently to what you think, what you do and how you behave. You gather about you strong people who, with you, will constantly agitate for change and difference. You strive to be today's benchmark of leadership excellence while planning to redefine excellence for tomorrow's. You identify those who are stretching beyond what convention suggests are limits in their field of endeavour, and find opportunity to share their experience. It is at this stage people you have led or influenced feature strongly in your learning and mentoring network.

And most importantly, you know that every moment brings the possibility to learn something, to fine tune your leadership effectiveness. You listen even more now for mood and for what motivates. Because people may not always volunteer these moments, it is a great leader who develops the kind of relationships that give you freedom to ask advice or feedback from anyone inside or outside the organisation. So, in talking with the cleaners, the ground staff, the supporters, the superstars, the senior staff, the opposition's coaches or whoever, there is input to the making of great leadership.

Dynasty or Leadership Consultant

While consolidating a quality leadership dynasty you enjoy respect for your understanding of leadership. The previous years find out the people who not only will become role models for leadership excellence, but who now have a deep understanding of what great leadership is all about. More than that, such key features as decision making are now appreciated for their value in general terms – across disciplines, sports, business and so on.

Even while continuing to exercise your senior leadership skills for your organisation your advice is sought as a leadership counsellor. You become a leadership solutions expert because you can recognise patterns and connections. Such leaders have developed what I might describe as a 'da Vinci' mindset. They readily apply both sides of their brains in understanding the bigger picture for other leaders whatever their field of endeavour. Because they also know the particular areas of expertise which other top leaders possess and are in regular contact with them as occasional advisors, they have learned to 'join up the dots' that such experts represent to create the best solutions.

Renaissance or Sage Mentor

Kevin Spacey[10] said, *'when you get to the top, you must remember to send the elevator back down'*. The leader must do that if leadership is to continue to grow. Just as you needed mentoring and access to advice on your career journey, you must now provide mentoring for those who will follow. The knowledge and experience you have accumulated will not always be seen as important to you, but to the mentee, it may be gold dust! You are a

To lead people, walk beside them.... As for the best leaders, the people do not notice their existence, the next best, the people honour and praise. The next, the people fear; and the next, the people hate.... When the best leader's work is done the people say, 'We did it ourselves!'

Lao-Tzu[11]

Leadership cannot really be taught. It can only be learned.

Harold Geneen[12]

Many ideas grow better when transplanted into another mind than in the one where they sprung up.

Oliver Wendell Holmes[13]

concepts connector who really understands why each bit of the bigger picture fits where it does.

The mentoring relationship should be learned and worked at so that not only the conscious intelligence resource is accessed, but there is also opportunity to learn from the subconscious resource of those things the mentor does from 'gut feelings'. Not all leaders find it easy to be a mentor, so advice on this should be sourced and embraced. This last stage in your journey completes the loop. The person being mentored becomes the mentor. A leadership legacy is established.

An Image of Quality Leadership

To conclude this chapter on leadership, I would like to describe my picture of what leadership looks like. The picture does not come from sport nor does it come from business, but I believe it does not stretch the imagination to see that it applies to both.

I think of a leader like the conductor of a great orchestra and choir. Imagine yourself as that conductor. You know the musical score and in your mind you hear the most beautiful outcome. You know what instruments and voices are required and select the musicians, choristers and soloists who will create that beauty. You cannot play any of the instruments as well as the musicians. Some you cannot play at all, nor can you sing as well as the choir members. You know each of the people you will lead has been trained well for their role. You have ensured that is the case. You know all will have studied and practiced their particular role not only in the orchestra but for this particular piece of music.

You know that in the performance none can hear the input of all other sections of the orchestra or choir. They are focused on the excellence of their personal contribution and in working with others in their section of the orchestra or choir. They trust you to ensure role excellence delivery from every person involved. They read their own music in front of them and play or sing to the lead you give. Each owns their individual performance.

The beauty you seek is an excellence of harmony and it is you who feels its balance. Someone good enough to be a soloist cannot have license to be so strong in their input that they disturb the harmony. The genius of every musician and singer is liberated to generate that harmony from the first to the final note you lead them through.

And in the end the whole beauty of this work goes beyond what you had heard in your mind and brings the audience to its feet in going beyond the horizons of their expectation. That is wonderful leadership.

Chapter 4

DECISIONS, DECISIONS

Right decisions are made by the right people at the right time. There is a sense of process and discipline to decision making. However, pressure of time in making decisions introduces a critical perspective for considering analysis versus intuition in terms of balance of influence in a process which includes implementation of the decision.

Decisions and Timeframes

Decision making does not end with the decision, but with its implementation, with action. In broad terms, given that the decisions we are talking about are important in their consequence, it seems to me that there are three types of decision characterised by their level of urgency and the time available to make them.

The first is where the decision must be made in the blink of an eye and the right action taken so quickly it appears reflexive. It also includes those 'executive' decisions that are made under extreme time pressure, so assessing other opinion is neither a reasonable nor realistic possibility.

The second is where there is opportunity to examine, or gather then examine the relevant advice and intelligence to make a considered decision then translate it into effective action personally or through others. Action

Be willing to make decisions.
That's the most important quality
in a good leader.

General George S. Patton[1]

Each player must accept the cards
life deals him or her; but once they are
in hand, he or she alone must decide how
to play the cards in order
to win the game.

Voltaire[2]

Life is the sum of all our choices.

Albert Camus[3]

Making decisions is the ability to
anticipate and to trust your instincts.

Gerhard Berger[4]

may be executed over a period of time to its completion, or immediately. There are clear timeframes in terms of deadline for making the mainstream decision.

The third is where there is considerable involvement of other people, not only in intelligence gathering and arriving at the decision, but in ensuring buy-in and commitment to delivery of the decision in practice. While there may be a date for announcing the decision there is normally enough time available to accommodate the size of this challenge. Here we are getting into 'the big stuff.'

In a Blink

In practice, the first situation is what the striker faces in front of the goal, or the tennis player receiving first service. It also covers the surgeon in moments of crisis in theatre, or staff in a safety alert on an oil rig, or emergency manoeuvres when driving. Being equipped to make right decisions here is founded on having the right extensive specific training and persistent learning both through personal experience and by input from experts. There is an intensity to the training and learning as each step of the performance build process (see Chapter 10) is revisited again and again. Pressure decisions, and delivering the consequent right and effective action under pressure must be practiced under pressure. This underlines the importance of steps 5 and 6 (pages 200-203) in the performance build process. It also highlights that having access to and learning from a great coach or master is essential.

Gerhard Berger suggested that the key to making such decisions in Formula 1 racing *is the ability to anticipate and to trust your instincts*. This is, of course, the outcome of experience specific to your role or function.

You become faster and faster at 'joining up the dots' of a situation and what needs to happen; then calling the shots almost instinctively. Some would, like Malcolm Gladwell or Gerd Gigerenzer, call it 'gut feeling' because in those moments it seems likely that decision making rests more in the territory of subconscious intelligence (see also Chapter 8 Coaches Intuition). I believe that this plays an increasing role in all decision making over time.

Nevertheless, as soon as is possible following such decision, there should be opportunity to review the decision; why it has been taken, what other options might have worked/not worked and so on. I think it should become a personal discipline to record this information as a cumulative decision making database.

Mainstream Decisions

The second type covers situations where there is time for conscious rational analysis of factors which will influence the decision. They include professional decisions such as those of GP's and consultants in medicine or of mechanics fixing the engine of your car or coaches changing the team's game plan at half time. They might be personal decisions such as what to do with your disposable income, or to change your weekly schedule to include regular exercise.

In fact, this type covers the majority of decisions that we make on a regular basis. Some come with the territory of change; some are part of our role in an organisation or in family life on a daily, weekly, monthly or other periodic basis. Only in the most exceptional of cases do those decisions not impact on others. We are all, then, decision makers. The quality of life we each enjoy and help others to enjoy has much to do with the quality of our decision making or as Albert Camus stated, *'life is the sum of all our choices'*. For the most part in our lives, I believe we are pretty good at making those decisions.

So how do we do it?

Well, Spock, Captain James T Kirk's Vulcan colleague on the Starship Enterprise in the TV series 'Star Trek' and Sheldon in 'The Big Bang Theory', would consider it a hyper-rational logical process, they would agree with these five steps.

1. Climate
Create a climate where effective decisions are possible. Because there is no consistent approach to making important choices, you must ensure that the right people are involved in the process. Creative thinking and careful deliberation should fuel their input. How the decision will be made must be agreed from the outset and the outcome should find each person enjoying a sense of involvement in it.

2. Define
What is the nature of the matter requiring the decision? There must be a clear understanding of the issues surrounding the matter and how each will affect the objectives of team, department and organisation; the equilibrium and wellbeing of the family, etc.

3. Options
What is the range of options or alternative courses of action available to address the matter? If there are no choices, what is there to be decided?

4. Assess
Which option is best? Feasibility, risks, advantages and consequences all must be considered for each option. A

range of excellent software can help enrich intelligence to be considered.

5. Decide

Make the decision building in the action plan. If there is a stalemate at this point, where the right decision is not clear for all who have been working on it, you must review options again, also checking if there were options or hybrids of options that were missed. As crunch time approaches when the decision is to be made you must call your shot even when others are still undecided, they should be comfortable that your call reflects their involvement.

At this point my advice is to see the options you are choosing from as photos that are in focus or out of focus. If one is in focus go for it. If none are in focus and:-

The decision can be postponed

Take time away from the matter completely, go though the process again, concentrating on best options and creating hybrids. Get others involved to construct arguments for the options they favour less and against those they favour more. If a clear focus emerges, go for it.

The decision cannot be postponed

Take the one in best focus and implement it as a starting point. Build in a tight monitoring system to find the point where the matter can be reviewed from a better or different perspective.

In all of this, there will be many occasions when making no decision or sticking to what's worked until now seems the easy option. But that's not the right option for credible and respected decision makers. Certainly it's not an option you would, as a leader, choose. You may not consciously choose to go through these five steps yet you will follow its sense of process. You will exercise your own discipline that will take you systematically to the point where the decision is made. Far more often than not, your decision will be the right one.

Tough decisions will take you to the edge of risk and adrenaline will pump through your system at these times. It takes real courage to step beyond that edge. That's a defining characteristic of great decision makers and, therefore, great leaders. To go to the edge then beyond is, of course, a matter of choice. It is one of the biggest decisions of anyone who leads. As a leader you have made it yours.

But none of us is a Spock, nor a Sheldon. We are human and we have our sensitivities and sensibilities! We have both emotional and intellectual intelligence. We think both ethically and logically. Our decisions are both about doing the right things and doing things right.

So in addition to the five steps process, most of us will consider another set of questions when making a decision. These have been accommodated in an acronym **RIGHT** created by Roger Steare in his book Ethicability.[5] When some decisions are to be made and which may create a moral dilemma, these questions should be considered.

Rules	What are the rules, regulations, laws the decision must comply with?
Integrity	How does the decision fit within our framework of core values and principles?
Good	Who will benefit from this decision and how?

Harm	Who could be damaged, hurt or disadvantaged by the decision and how?
Truth	In this decision, are we being honest and accountable?

Back on the 'Enterprise', Captain Kirk was the leader and decision maker, not Spock. His decisions took account of Spock's logic, of course, but they also applied the Captain's human value judgements because they involved people. And that's how you and I make our decisions. We are aware that decision making is as much an art as it is a science. Life according to G.K. Chesterton[6] *'is a trap for logicians....... Its wildness lies in wait'*.

The science is a consideration of the relevant knowledge that is brought to bear on the decisions we must make and applying the discipline of process. The art is in our style and effectiveness in identifying and connecting what needs to be done with the best option, then calling the shot and delivering. Developing that art comes down to two things; quality of practice, and making the right decision on who to coach us in our development.

So what does this look like when it comes to a key decision moment:

On January 15, 2009 US Airways flight 1549 took off from New York La Guardia airport at 15.25 (EST) for Charlotte North Carolina. First Officer Jeffrey B Skiles was at the controls and this was his first flight in the Airbus A320 since passing the training course for this type of aircraft. Two minutes after take off the aircraft collided with a flock of Canada Geese, many of which were ingested by the engines, causing an immediate loss of all thrust. What happened next was a rich mix of what goes into 'in a blink' and 'mainstream' decisions. Captain Chesley Sullenberger took the controls as Skiles went through the three page checklist of emergency procedures to try and restart the engines.

Sullenberger had been a US Airforce fighter pilot and was a glider pilot and safety expert. Since leaving the Airforce in 1980, he had been an airline pilot. Although La Guardia and Teterboro airports gave landing permission, Sullenberger told air traffic controllers 'we can't do it'. He then called the shot 'we're gonna be in the Hudson' (river). The safety of his passengers and the citizens of New York was the clear objective, yet the manoeuvre itself carried extreme risk. For example, the aircraft would pass less than 270 metres above the George Washington Bridge; and the angle of the aircraft to the water on landing, if only a few degrees out, would cause the aircraft to break up.

Four minutes after colliding with the birds, the aircraft was landed safely in the Hudson River. All 155 passengers and crew survived the landing and were safely evacuated including a passenger in a wheelchair. Thanks to the work of the cabin crew and the immediate response, first by Captains Brittany Catanzaro and Vincent Lombardi commanding the N.Y. Waterway Ferries, the first of their vessels arrived four minutes after the aircraft ditched. N.Y. City Fire and Police Departments followed within minutes, plus a privately owned Coastguard buoy tender. There were only two serious injuries among the 75 people treated, five were treated for hypothermia. (The Hudson water temperature was 2°C, air temperature −7°C.)

Even in the evacuation Sullenberger was calling critical shots. He advised ferry crews to rescue passengers on the wing before those in the inflatable slides, as the latter provided a higher level of safety. Having twice walked the length of the cabin to check that no one was inside the

Experience is a hard teacher, because she gives the test first and the lesson afterwards.

Vernon Law[7]

Experience is one thing you can't get for nothing.

Oscar Wilde[8]

Some choices we live not only once but a thousand times over, remembering them for the rest of our lives.

Richard Bach[9]

plane following the evacuation, Sullenberger was the last to leave the aircraft.

It is the cumulative experiences in our lives that we draw upon in lesser or greater measure to make decisions. That they are the right decision is balanced at the edge of risk. Captain Chesley 'Sully' Sullenberger is some equilibrist!

Into the Big Stuff

The third type of decision is probably only for those who aspire to, or who are already in, senior leadership roles. These decisions concern substantial change of some sort, affecting parts of organisations, or organisations themselves. They are at the culture change, strategic framework design level. The defining characteristic which sets high performing organisations apart is the ability of their leaders to make the right decisions and make them happen quickly. The tone in this is set by the senior leadership, and they do so by addressing the following basic principles.

- **Prioritise decisions that build value in the organisation.**

  These may be in the area of major decisions of strategy, but they may also lie in the area of operational decisions at the sharp end of things.

- **Buy-in is the result you need.**

  The decision is incomplete without consequent effective action. People shape the decision and people deliver the action. They are far stronger in their commitment to both if they feel involved. So it's not just their agreement that must be worked for, but their buy-in: it's not just their heads and hands, it's their hearts.

- **It's the right people who make right decisions.**

For each decision making position throughout the organisation it is essential to select the right people in the right part of the organisation at the right level and the right time. Different situations will often require different decision makers so there must be an acceptance of occasional territorial flexibility.

- **Clarity is essential in making people accountable.**

In the decision making process, those responsible for constructive input, for making the decision and for putting the decision into action must be identified and their roles clearly defined.

- **The organisation must support and reinforce the principles set out here.**

In the context of 'Winning Matters', the principles make the **O**wn, **D**ecide, **D**o concept happen (see page 7) but only if the organisation's culture supports its people and engages with them in practice.

- **Grow and regularly use a network of people with different expertise, or who think differently.**

Right intelligence is essential to making right decisions. Knowing and having access to those with experience and expertise to generate that intelligence is paramount. This may mean going outside a department or even the organisation. To

enrich the process in practice and for diversity of input, the network this represents should include a lateral thinking group.

- **Those who will live in it should be involved in building it.**

A big motivator to making decisions work and to making change happen is being involved in the thinking behind it and being part of the decision making process.

- **Adapt fast or die.**

No matter how well thought through, decisions may have to be reviewed as conditions and circumstances change once the decision is implemented. There has to be an agility in making and in reviewing decisions commensurate with the accelerating speed of change in business, in sport and in life. For all decisions made and implemented, there must be a process in place to learn from them, and respond fast to adjust when necessary. In fact, getting the right people together, to make right decisions at speed gives an organisation a huge winning edge.

In summary, whatever the type of decision to be made, once all facts are known in the matter we must not only manage the necessary balance between rational process and agreed values frameworks, but also between conscious and subconscious intelligence; between analysis and intuition. Fortunately the intellect informs both. When we make decisions it's not an 'either/ or' affair, it is invariably a bit of both. Or, as Peter Senge concluded:

'People with high levels of personal mastery cannot afford to choose between reason and intuition, or head and heart, anymore than they would choose to walk on one leg or see with one eye'.[10]

Chapter 5

PREPARED TO LEARN

As the dust settles from the bruising encounter of this arena, you have already started your journey towards the next. Your future performance will be determined by learning all you can from this one, and turning it into effective action. To learn fast from each moment of this encounter, you must prepare yourself to do so. This is about creating a system for persistent monitoring, review and learning.

Tomorrow Began Yesterday

The first step from the podium in today's competitive arena is the first step towards the podium in tomorrow's. That step is in the right direction when you have learned all you can from the competition, applied that learning to guide the next step, then consigned today's arena to history. No matter if today's outcome is perceived as triumph or disaster, no matter if athlete and team feel elated or bruised, everything we squeeze from the experience must generate the energy of motivation to create competitive advantage for the next arena.

We must know why we win - or it is an accident and we learn nothing from the experience about how to win next time. We must be prepared to be tough in review even when there is no apparent pressure to do so. We must know why we have not won, or we are condemned to repeat that fate again and again. Failure isn't persistent provided we learn from those moments when things don't work out the way we planned.

If we come from the podium of triumph and elation, we must work at how to ruthlessly extend and press home that advantage. We will continue to practice winning and permit the opposition to practice losing. We will leave them struggling with yesterday's mountains which are the bench marks of an excellence we established yesterday, while we move on to invent new benchmarks that will be tomorrow's mountains. Some people think that being in the lead is tough because you don't have an opponent to measure yourself against. But, again, like Usain Bolt in seeking to improve his own world records, you still have your own pacemaker out there: it's you.

If we come from the stumble of disaster and bruisings we are resilient in aggressively regaining ground we have lost and reducing any advantage the opposition think they may now have. We pace our forward fight to gain a true momentum. Our objective remains to be the best that we can be individually and together, personally and collectively. So, when we pass the opposition, as we surely will, we keep going. Again, like Bolt, going beyond the opposition's horizon is not what excellence or winning is for us: it's maintaining our own relentless pursuit of redefining personal excellence.

Such energy of motivation to go for the win next time is the same, whatever the result last time. It is given direction by what we have learned now through the quality of our review process and how we apply that to take us forward. This applies whether at conclusion of the 4 year Olympic cycle; the annual cycle; or the day to day, week to week cycle. The review must be executed immediately, before the heat is forgotten and passion evaporates; before passage of time brings false perception of events. It is really important to understand that from the post major event review through to the daily debriefing; this is the part of the event or day which launches us with advantage into the next. Don Shula made this clear. *'The game doesn't end with the final whistle on Sunday afternoon. It ends once you have learned all you can from the experience and done something about it.'* So he ensured that everyone, whether player or member of coaching and support staff, immediately and meticulously reviewed their personal and team performance as the basis of preparing for the next game.

Realignment

The four week period that follows an Olympic Games is not vacation time! It is when everything the chief coach needs to have learned from the experience of these games and the preparation for them must be reviewed in detail. The review must look at the strategy, plan or tactic that has been pursued; the people who have delivered it; and the people who designed, managed and led it. Everything and everyone comes under the microscope. *This time scale is about realigning strategy.*

The hours that follow a weekend match in a season's campaign, or days at the end of a season are the most critical to understanding and evaluating all that can be learned from the experience of this match or season against the background of those preceding it. The quality of decisions relative to individual and team performance preparation and execution in the next match or season are determined by how these hours or days are used. *This time scale is about realigning performance plans.*

The minutes that follow each day of a tournament or

**Success isn't permanent and
failure isn't fatal.**

Mike Ditka[1]

**The time to repair the roof is when the
sun is shining.**

John F Kennedy[2]

**He who is not ready today will be
less ready tomorrow.**

Ovid[3]

**I don't think you learn as much
from results as you do from achieving a
new level of performance or even when
falling short in the fight
to get there.**

Frank Dick

each daily workout are vital to evaluating each person's potential or the effect of the day to day program on those being trained and the efficiency of the training process. Monitoring and responding to each situation provides the intelligence required to constructively adjust the process. *This time scale is about realigning game plans.*

Different Arenas – Same Process

In principle, if not in all practical detail, there are clear and important parallels here, for business and, indeed, for our lives. In some instances it is simply the terminology that is different. For example, the processes involved in designing performance plans in sport are the same as in designing business plans in the commercial world.

A chief coach of an Olympic sport has at least four years to prepare athletes, teams and those who lead, develop, or support their endeavours through training and competition, for what amounts to a few defining moments in the brutal Olympic arena where there are no second chances. While timescales may vary from 1 to 4 years, it is a similar situation for non Olympic sports and their world championships and cups. Annually, for many sports, there are months of preparation before competition. Likewise this applies in those businesses where many months are devoted to preparation before the product or service offering is delivered. In these cases, preparation and delivering performance excellence under pressure are sequential.

This is not really the case for business in general, nor in a back to back competition situation in sports where there is virtually a year round season as for example, in Formula 1, PGA Tour or League Championships. Here, preparation and performance excellence under pressure run simultaneously. It is self evident that taking care of business is almost a daily, if not, an hourly affair. In this situation, by turning each moment to advantage we can influence the outcome in the arena we are in right now and enable colleagues to do so. Tomorrow's arena and those to follow must be prepared for by learning from today's and building what is learned into addressing different and more demanding levels of challenge tomorrow. That may be tough, but it is certainly possible.

In both sequential and simultaneous cases, we must establish a process for reviewing and learning on the move. We must live an agility in constantly learning, adjusting, adapting and moving things up a notch. Often, we will even change direction. This applies when preparing, when performing and when doing both.

Learning Faster

To win persistently, we must constantly apply that process. We must live that agility. The purpose of review is not about being judgmental as a prelude to some emotional outpouring or explosion. It is about learning fast. Why? Because, to quote Arie de Geus, *'probably the only sustainable competitive advantage we have, is the ability to learn faster than the opposition.'* Hence the need to review on the move and to be agile in this. We must create opportunity to seize that advantage from long term planning through to each moment in the arena.

Therefore the machinery for review must be put in place in advance of the event whether it is to learn faster in a match, from daily business, or an Olympic campaign. I cannot stress enough the importance of this. We must prepare to learn. We must create a strategy and a system, so that learning is possible from the first moments of the event. It is a mistake to have nothing in place to ensure that all lessons are captured.

Information Gather

When reviewing in sport, we review not only our own team but also that of crucial opposition this time and, proactively, those who may be crucial opposition next time.

The essential review headings in sport are:

- Results – intended and actual.

- Performance under pressure of athletes and teams.

- Professional competence of all staff – coaching, management, administration and performance support.

- Effectiveness of athlete and team staff in preparation planning.

- Effectiveness of overall campaign strategy/current year plan/applied game plan.

- Leverage of high performance intelligence and resources, e.g. systems and technology.

- Quality of chief coach decision making and judgment calls.

In business, what is learned through this process is not only relevant to overall strategy and the development and preparation of our people, but to what and how marketing is planned and executed. Input into what has been learned comes from everyone involved in, or associated with, the enterprise. That includes managers, coaches, athletes, administrators, performance and support staff, expert commentators and analysts, the sport's funding bodies and the sport committees and supporters who, after all, are our customers.

Again, in principle, it is similar in business. Just change some of the titles. Athletes and teams are staff and departments. Leaders, managers, administrators and coaches all exist in business. The board is the board and each business has its own shareholders and/or financial backers. The chief coach is leadership calling the shots. Customers are, well, customers!

The review needs to establish the knowledge base required to make the necessary decisions in designing our next performance plan or strategy. There are three very broad and obvious timescales when building a thorough and effective review process.

Longer Term Reviews
Strategy and business plans

The priority in addressing these points will depend on time-scales involved. All points are relevant for review in preparation for a 1 to 4 year strategy however, in my opinion there are six fundamental points in this.

1. Extrapolated numbers for winning results, performance and components of future performance.

2. Perceived successful technical training and tactical trends.

3. Effectiveness in preparation and in the arena.

4. Strengths and vulnerabilities.

5. What could be done differently and what different things can be done to perform better and gain competitive advantage next time.

6. Identify the people who will grow a winning dynasty.

Personal experience and expertise; continuous listening and learning; and the understanding and synthesis of the review outcome equips the chief coach to shape an action plan or strategy to achieve greater things when faced with the next competitive challenge. This will subsequently change in detail simply because you are continuously and quickly learning on the move. For the most part, the people who will execute the plan or strategy will also contribute to that reshaping. And, of course, the arena itself and the variables that impact getting us there, require a constant discipline to adjust, fine tune and occasionally even scrap things.

It is frequently the case in sport, business, the performing arts and across the professions that preparatory drafts of plans and strategies for future challenges are already well progressed before the present challenge has been addressed. In fact, where this happens, as recommended earlier, the machinery to review and to learn has been thought through and put in place in anticipation of the present challenge. Such machinery is designed to help the decision making that will refine the preparatory drafts. What must not happen, however, is that in drawing up such preparatory plans there is a robotic routine carry over of what has worked up until now.

It is the review quality and the understanding of its messages that dictate how future planning is shaped. Whether the strategic planning, action planning or any other planning has been commenced before or after we stepped into the present arena, there must be a sense of order to it. Broadly speaking, that order covers process for defining the goal, how to achieve it and how to learn from the experience to be better next time. I will discuss the idea of establishing such order within a planning framework or model in Chapter 9. In this chapter, however, I want to keep our eye on the ball of learning from the

Probably the only sustainable competitive advantage we have, is the ability to learn faster than the opposition.

Arie de Geus[4]

You have to learn the rules of the game. And then you have to play better than anyone else.

Albert Einstein[5]

Get over the idea that children should spend their time in study. Be a student so long as you still have something to learn, and this will mean all your life.

Henry L. Doherty[6]

Great ability develops and reveals itself increasingly with every new assignment.

Baltasar Gracián[7]

experience through review.

The speed at which the review is completed, relevant intelligence obtained, draft action plan or strategy designed and selection made, cannot compromise the quality of the processes involved nor outcomes sought. Demonstrating agility must accelerate us in our never ending journey towards personal and collective excellence. Highest quality execution of all aspects of the review processes must be meticulously adhered to; making sure nothing is left to chance.

Medium Term Reviews
World class performance plans in sport and business/marketing plans

The medium term reviews are from intra-season through to annual in sport; and from quarterly to annual in business. They apply variously to a launching pad for the next period; realignment with the annual plan, business plan or longer term strategy; to help shape preview for 'this time next year/season'; and, possibly more so than the shorter and longer term reviews, to create opportunity to celebrate and motivate.

They build on the day to day through to 6 weekly shorter term reviews. The larger slice of time provides a picture of the business itself and of different parts of the business in terms of progress towards the goals of an overall strategy; improvements against our own previous performance at this time of the year or in general; of where we are compared with the opposition at this point in the calendar; and so on. Importantly, they do so in a timescale that affords opportunity to make adjustments, corrections and improvements to get back on track where that is what's needed.

However, because, as already argued, delivering better personal performance is the winning difference in the arena, each person, in whatever their field of endeavour, should be reviewed as follows:-

Review criteria

1. What are the performance components relative to the person's role? (Key Performance Indicators - KPI's or Key Performance Determinants - KPD's).

2. What are the agreed standards for those components relative to the person's performance target?

3. What are the delivered/present standards in these components relative to the person's current performance?

4. When these match or are better than those agreed; recognise, appreciate and improve.

5. If these do not, diagnose problems and correct them.

6. What are the revised performance component standards?

In sport, the KPI's or KPD's are the technical, fitness and behavioural building blocks that need to be in place to deliver the performance required for a given sport, position in a team, etc. In business, they are what each role demands. In addition, I believe there is considerable value in exchanging randomly, but at least twice a year, a performance alignment check (PAC) (figure 5). This is where either the coach/line manager or the team member/ person being managed can contact each other and carry out the following process:-

1. The team member self assesses their own current performance and performance progress relative to the goals/objectives agreed at the annual performance review.

2. The coach also assesses the team member.

3. They exchange their completed assessments.

4. When there is agreement on things being on track or ahead of schedule then that is appreciated and progress continues.

5. When there is disagreement or where there is agreement on problems a meeting is called. Problems are discussed and addressed, and a plan agreed on how to get things back on course.

Figure 5

CONFIDENTIAL	
ORGANISATION:	**PERFORMANCE ALIGNMENT CHECK**
Informal Performance Review **Period of review:**_____	**Overall role performance rating** **(10 max – 1 min)**
Name _____ Prepared by :_____	Role: _____ Date: _____

Significant changes influencing role during the period under review	Effect on performing role	
Prioritised objectives set at commencement of year under review	Evaluation of objective achievement	Rating Notes
Prioritized agreed main tasks to meet objectives	Main task performance analysis	Rating Notes
Strengths/developments	Suggested action required for improvement	

Hide not your talents, they were for use made. What's a sun dial in the shade?

Benjamin Franklin[8]

Man's mind, once stretched by a new idea, never regains its original dimensions.

Oliver Wendell Holmes[9]

Arriving at one goal is the starting point to another.

John Dewey[10]

This ensures timely intervention to keep personal performance and, therefore, team performance on track. It is strongly recommended that this process is informal and is not a matter of permanent record. It is, quite simply, a coaching aid. At the end of a season, year, or campaign, the PAC concept can be very effective when applied prior to that formal portion of review which focuses on personal performance of each member of the team or business.

Shorter Term Reviews
Game plans and tactics

The shorter term reviews, compiled from reading the game during play as a team member or coach, are actually the basic building blocks of the entire review process. They make up the essential mosaic of learning through experience that is the backdrop to future continuous excellence. They also ensure that what is working now is turned to even greater advantage and what is not is swiftly corrected.

Think of it this way, if you get a stone in your shoe in the first mile of the marathon, when do you take it out? Pretty quick, or you'll under-perform for the rest of the race! The shortest term are the post match analyses and reviews, daily and weekly debriefs in business, half time feedback and assessment, or briefing during pit stops and so on.

The broad areas covered reflect the immediate performance priorities. The intelligence obtained must be readily translated into action that produces better performance in very tight time scales. The detail is, naturally, very specific, but the following is a simple, easily adapted and relatively quick to execute process at a general level in team or individual sports; or team level in business.

Team debrief
1. Were we on target in terms of result?

2. What helped performance?

3. What did not help performance?

4. What can we use to our advantage from 2 and 3?

5. What worked this time and can we build on that?

6. What did not work this time and can we correct that or eliminate it?

7. What will we do differently and better?

8. What different things will we do?

9. What will we stop doing?

Next, over 4 to 6 week cycles there is focus on the individual. This again is readily adapted to meet the specifics of a given role.

Individual debrief
1. What is the performance target?

2. What tasks are required to achieve the performance?

3. What actions are carried out to complete the task?

4. What is the current performance?

5. If it exceeds the target; recognise, appreciate and improve farther.

6. If it is below target, diagnose problems and correct.

7. What is the revised performance target?

A variation of the PAC concept can also have immense value in the context of shorter term interviews. For several years now, the very successful Ipswich Town Football Club Academy has encouraged young players to pursue a self assessment routine after a game. They score their personal performance in passing, tackling, moving off the ball, etc, out of 10 for each skill, then discuss this with a member of the coaching staff. The idea is that, irrespective of how the team performs, we each have to be accountable for stepping up to the mark in the game. We can each do something similar in our own lives. Even if this is not done every game or every day in our several arenas, it should be done from time to time to check how well we are delivering on our accountability.

It has not been my intention here to make an apotheosis of review and measurement. Rather, it is to argue the importance of being in the best possible position to learn faster how to perform better so that we can be more effective in all those arenas that make up our life. The more frequently we do so, the less time it takes.

> *Never leave today without having put everything in place to make tomorrow's performance count.*

Then, having done so, walk away, regenerate so that tomorrow you hit a winning rhythm from the outset. That way you are in the regular business of getting things right; rather than wasting time and energy trying to put things right and compromising your drive to remain a winner.

Chapter 6

PEOPLE CHOICE

Whether leading a team, or being part of a team, we need the right people doing the right thing on our side. So selection of the best people is the first priority if we are to be successful in our endeavour. This is not about what they have achieved, but what we will achieve today and what we will continue to achieve in tomorrow's very different arenas.

Selection Criteria

It is the ability to make the right decisions and judgement calls that separates the great from the average in all walks of life. In all of the planning and preparation to win and keep on winning, the decisions made in selecting the best people to ensure that we do so, are, without doubt, the most important. When starting from scratch or when circumstance obliges you to replace people in an organisation, or when selecting people for a new project, selection criteria can be summarised as:

Technical Ability
Select first on the basis of how well their strengths and specific skills fit the role you are selecting for and the goals you seek to achieve. Now that is pretty obvious stuff, but it is absolutely essential to get it right. The entire enterprise must be founded on the right people with the

right skills and fitness to do the job. A mistake here means you are building on a flawed foundation. Excellence in the required skills is a given and the person selected must hit all the right measures of fitness. With athletes this means strength, explosive power, endurance, and most importantly, speed. Whether or not the person is in form or recovering from injury or being out of form also needs to be considered

Coachability
Now I know that word won't be found in the dictionary, but you know what it means. You need the people you select to be hungry to listen, learn and grow personally and as team players, in response to their leaders, coaches and colleagues.

Balance
There are three dimensions to this.

First you must have, between the people you are selecting, the full range and diversity of skills to achieve your goal. That means in rugby you do not select fifteen full backs! So balance in this context is assuring the necessary diversity of technical abilities bound by a unity of purpose. This will often mean you are looking for players with skills that are in addition to those necessary for their role/position. This opens the door to expanding the options for how the team may play and raise its game.

Next, balance is about having people who can maintain or recover balance in pursuit of the goal when conditions or circumstance contrive to knock their endeavour off balance. So you are looking here for flexibility in what they do and versatility in how they do it.

Finally, there is balance which comes from personal discipline in keeping all variables in their life well managed within a strong framework of shared core values. This is

Regardless of how you feel inside, always try to look like a winner. Even if you are behind, a sustained look of control and confidence can give you a mental edge that results in victory.

Arthur Ashe[1]

Be careful of players in the team who never make mistakes; and those who make the same mistake twice.

Frank Dick

Look for people who will aim for the remarkable, who will not settle for the routine.

David Ogilvy[2]

fundamental to a team player. It is about understanding their role as being like a component in the equilibrium of a suspended mobile. One component out of place disrupts the entire system. To deliver role excellence in the team, each player must know and contribute to the dynamic of its equilibrium. In doing so, they will persistently get the best out of themselves for the team.

Chemistry

Qualities under this heading are the unique parts of the person's character. They are those traits that make them different and special. People don't make winning possible for themselves or their team because of their sameness, but because of their difference. Character, to me, is not a label but the sum of those individual qualities a person brings to any given situation (see pages 125 - 126). It embraces qualities such as ambition, pride and empathy, willingness to challenge and enjoy being challenged, past record of performing under pressure, personality type and so on. Often they are bundled together to create a picture of a person's attitude. Much of this is assessed these days through instruments such as psychometrics. There is a large element here, however, that comes in the territory of things that you can feel but can't touch. So, in my opinion, you must also be willing to exercise judgement calls based on your experience and intuition or, quite simply on gut feel. It is important that we each learn to be efficient at 'reading people'.

Will to Win

That's just what it says on the label. You must feel you are looking into the eyes of winners. You must feel that they want to win, believe they will win and will persist until they do win for the team and for themselves. They exude a commitment to team and personal excellence. On the one hand they radiate a sense that the team will make a winning difference to them in their own growth and development. They believe in your ability to lead it; and that they will get coaching and support to be the winner they want to be. On the other hand they radiate a sense that they will fight to be all that they must be to ensure that their team is a winning team.

Rebuilding Teams

It is not often we have the luxury of starting from scratch. Mostly, we are rebuilding after review. There are two timescales in such review, constant churn and periodic.

Constant Churn Selection
The first timescale is review after each situation where challenges are in frequent succession and where there is a pool of people to choose from. This might be through the regular season for sports teams; a run of a West End show; a hospital operating team; rapidly occurring projects in business, and so on.

Here, selection is made from those already in the pool or organisation on the basis of the above criteria. Now, however, a tighter focus is applied through additional criteria – the '6 F's'.

• Fitness
In sport and in business this starts with skills that are robust, effective and sharp. Here, fitness becomes pretty specific in terms of strength and endurance according to the demands of the role and situation. On this foundation, the critical fitness component is speed. Of course, in sport that is both speed of co-ordination, or across the ground, plus speed of reaction or response to testing situations. Outside sport there are parallels but most important is

being fit to be part of, or to increase, that rhythm of team operation that produces winning performance. In an ideal world, such fitness parameters should be constantly monitored in training and in the pressure of competition to help decision making in this aspect of selection.

• Form
It is unrealistic to believe that any of us can be at the top of our form 100% of the time. Yet the team has to deliver a winning performance on a regular basis. It is for this reason that the cycle of pressure versus regeneration, of pushing to the limit versus recovery, is not the same for everyone in the team in terms of timing. While varying the cycle helps ensure that teams avoid huge fluctuations in performance, there will still be times when a particular performer gets a form slump. Many organisations now encourage some form of stress monitoring to spot potential slump. Mostly, form can be restored quickly with a change in training, a regeneration program or a review of overall lifestyle including what we eat and drink.

I believe every one of us can have the occasional period of off colour performance whatever our role in the organisation. So you will understand my strong recommendation for all of us to have our stress levels monitored and that we each pursue a personal performance and development plan with inbuilt regeneration. If form slumps extend into longer periods of more than two to three weeks health and wellbeing advice should be sought.

• Fight
This is not just about hunger to get into the heat of battle and to prove they are the right person for the job: it is about their record of mental toughness (see page 209). In particular, it is about consistency in handling pressure

when asked to step up to the plate. Related to this is the delicate judgement that must be exercised when considering the appropriate time to replace the older, wiser, reliable member of the team with the younger, energy packed but less experienced. Sometimes the former brings moments of genius that come from incredible mental sharpness, and which change the game; sometimes they have the game played in a way that accommodates reduced physical sharpness. Sometimes the latter outpaces and out energises the opposition; sometimes their inexperience is costly.

It is a wise coach who makes that judgement call before it has to be made. This comes down to knowing your people, understanding the people business and putting the team first.

• Fit in

This is a difficult criterion to measure. It is the person's capacity to fit with the team. Often fitting in is less about the technical skills that a player has and where they enhance or compliment the collective competence of the team. Rather, it is about their influence off the field as much as on it. Great players may sometimes not be fully in control of their egos and can be rough diamonds (see page 104) whose rough edges can do a bit of damage to those around them. This may not be too much of a problem in those teams where people do not have to cooperate with each other or work together. In these cases, the players get on with their own thing, achieving the target contributions they must achieve for the collective performance of the overall team. It is a problem, however, when it compromises the team dynamic in situations where cohesion is essential. Reinforcing the values that embrace the team dynamic and which help one 'fit in' is what has motivated even the strongest of team excellence organisations to take on board team building events.

• Flexibility

This refers to the extra skills a player brings to the team which enhance its versatility potential. By that I do not simply mean technically, but behaviourally. So the enhancement is what the team can now do that it couldn't without this person and how they can be more effective in their style of play. In sport this can embrace everything from specialist skills, through creativity, to character to influence and motivate. It can also refer to the dimension of play to which a team may need access in order to deal with the unique challenge that an arena or an opposition represents. Naturally, a team needs to play to its strengths. Very occasionally the team may also have to raise the level or priority of negotiating, or negating the opposition's strengths.

• Forward

This includes:

- Preparing the new kids on the block for their role in future winning teams. A strategy should be in place for when they are afforded the learning opportunity of the big arenas.
- The ongoing campaign means that selection must ensure a balance of winning potential throughout. So if there is a bigger challenge four weeks from now, compared to this week, selection must take care of business on both occasions, any others between, and for the rest of the campaign. Team quality consistency is the key: select accordingly.
- Players coming back from absence due to injury, following a rest or after a form slump need to be carefully re-introduced to the team. Careful consideration must be given to when the player is brought back into the game. Speed of co-ordination or across the ground; and speed of response or

decision making may be rusty, so the player should be brought on only after the rhythm of play has settled to a slower pace. There also has to be the understanding of other players and indeed a patience, when the returning player or even new, young players to this level of game, pressure and rhythm, may get their timing wrong when speed of response and co-ordination don't match. The key here is to manage expectations of everyone in the team and those coming back or being introduced.

Finally, those selecting the team must be constantly aware of the need to keep the motivational climate strong for everyone in the selection pool all the time. That starts with ensuring selection policy and decision making have only one focus – the winning quality of the team. The underlying mood throughout the pool must be that the team selected is made greater because everyone of us is great. A winning team remains that way because everyone in the pool is so well prepared to deliver performance excellence, that the selectors have both a very tough and a very easy job! The 6 F's are relevant to business teams and sports teams alike.

Periodic selection
For the second timescale, in sport this can be during transfer periods, season/campaign end or following major events such as an Olympics or World Cup. The purpose is to maintain the highest quality of team performance in arenas where the performance standards required to deliver the results we aim for are constantly being raised. Those selected then represent the pillar around which the next strategy, team performance plan and game plans will be built. These decisions are made on the basis of

the five selection criteria listed at the beginning of this chapter but there are some tough issues to take into account.

Surely the situation is no different in business. Although timescales might vary, the challenge of maintaining highest levels of team performance must be addressed. Periodic reviews provide a basis for doing so. I believe that this should definitely happen at least annually when we not only review the business plan but also everyone involved in its delivery.

I find it is useful to apply this simple diagram as a starting point for grading people A-D (figure 6).

Figure 6

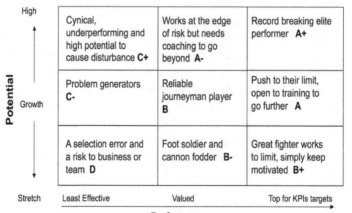

POTENTIAL AND PERFORMANCE

	Least Effective	Valued	Top for KPIs targets
High	Cynical, underperforming and high potential to cause disturbance **C+**	Works at the edge of risk but needs coaching to go beyond **A-**	Record breaking elite performer **A+**
Growth	Problem generators **C-**	Reliable journeyman player **B**	Push to their limit, open to training to go further **A**
Stretch	A selection error and a risk to business or team **D**	Foot soldier and cannon fodder **B-**	Great fighter works to limit, simply keep motivated **B+**

Performance

A = Retain at all costs, leaders to watch and stretch
B = Keep if you can and develop
C = Improve or lose
D = Help make them happier in another team that fits their skill set

Potential and performance
- **A Players**

  In sport there will be athletes, coaches, support staff etc. who perform in and for the present team and who will continue in the team or make individual challenges to make the team next time. They constitute the building blocks of experience and elite performance on which team excellence will be founded given continued commitment and development. These we identify through the review as A members.

- **B Players**

  There will be those who perform well in the present team and whose potential and current performance, given the right personal preparation planning and their determination to be winners, will provide immense return on training investment in them. They are identified through the review as B members now.

- **C/D Players**

  Finally, there will be a clearly identified group who currently under perform even without being under pressure and/or whose motivational life appears to have entered the twilight zone. They are C and D members. It is important here to differentiate between ability and performance. We all have different strengths across our range of abilities. Our personal development is to improve on our abilities both where we are strong and not so strong so that we can perform better and contribute more to the team. In our teams we will have a range of ability, so some players are at a level where they can contribute more than others. This is not what determines an A, B or C player. Rather it is their performance in developing and delivering their abilities. It is their capacity to deliver a performance which truly reflects their potential.

  In European Cup athletics, the maximum points an athlete could score in an event was 8. Someone who is worth 1 point on paper yet delivers 2 gives us the same advantage as someone worth 5 giving 6. C players more often than not under-perform in delivering their abilities in contributing to team advantage. They might be worth 6 points on paper but only occasionally perform at that level. When it comes to decision making on whom to retain or release, the issue of how potential versus performance is dealt with must be clearly understood.

For example, if one player is in your team at present because they have 8 point ability yet repeatedly produce 4; and another has one point ability yet through training and commitment delivers 3; it is tempting to retain the former because 4 is better than 3! On the other hand, the former is currently costing you 4 where the latter is giving you 2 and, given further training, may produce more than 4! Sometimes the person who should be your number one player is a C performer. Your coaching here will focus on attitude change. If that doesn't happen then find a replacement. D players persistently under perform and have little potential to do better.

People Development Tactics

As a guide to tactics where it comes to helping a player towards upward mobility, whether A, B, C or D, I think of it as set out in figure 7. Some conversations with C players (and all with D) are not really enjoyable affairs. It is essential, however, that they achieve the purpose for which performance review meetings are called without undue stress on both sides. So:-

- Go for the ball, not the player. The discussions are not personal attacks, they are about specific examples of underperformance.

- Get to the solution through a real personal communication which means face to face. E-communication is not acceptable.

- Plan the meeting detail, from content to where chairs are placed.

- Cover all relevant points and check that all are understood. It is worth writing down each input and response.

- Agree actions to be taken including timescales and when you will next meet to review progress.

- Follow up in writing.

- Ensure a stress free environment before, during and after the meeting. So avoid the possibility of the person having to pass amongst colleagues en route to the meeting and after it.

When making decisions on what kind of coaching the C or D player needs, I find the questions set out in figure 8 useful checklist. That final question - 'are they perverse?' leads me to the world of what some refer to as 'rough diamonds'.

Rough Diamonds

To me, everyone is precious in a team whoever they are and whatever their role. Each has real value and each of us must identify, recognise and appreciate that value. Each of us likes to feel valued and must ensure that all team members are.

It is often the case, however, that these 'precious as diamonds' people are not perfect fits in the team. They are like 'rough diamonds'. The diamond part sparkles and is normally easily recognised. Some of the 'rough' bits are exciting and constructive, bringing an extra edge/dimension of advantage. On the other hand, some of the rough bits can make them different to the point of being difficult, even in teams where all have well developed skills in managing diversity.

The rough bits must, then, be identified and their positive or negative influence understood then used to advantage or carefully handled to avoid damage both to the person and to the team. When action is indicated, I think there are six steps to coping with the Rough Diamond (RD) situation.

Figure 7

PERFORMANCE	TACTIC
Persistently below the line	6 week management up to 3 times (18 weeks) maximum
Below the line	Encourage change and design 6 week controlled coaching programme
On the line	Raise the bar to lift aspiration and work level through a 6 week partnership coaching programme 'get ready to fly'
Above the line	Set stretch challenges to go for the top and be there to coach if needed
Well above the line	Re-define excellence – design a competence expansion plan and prepare for promotion

Figure 8

Is the task clear?	Do they understand the task and what excellence looks like?
Is task importance/urgency clear?	Do they understand why their performance of the task matters?
Is this the right person for the task?	Do they have skills to perform the task and is it suited to their role?
Is the environment right?	Are we managing the environment to eliminate perceived obstacles and afford appropriate support?
Is our response appropriate?	Are we helping them to learn the right lessons?
Is our feedback loop complete?	Are we providing timely and consistent coaching and feedback?
Are they perverse?	Have we let them know such behaviour has no place here – and the consequences of repetition?

*Trust men and they will be true to you;
treat them greatly and they will show
themselves great.*

Ralph Waldo Emerson[3]

*It is by your decisions that others
measure who you really are,
not by your actions, nor by
their consequences.*

Frank Dick

*The secret is to work less as individuals
and more as a team.
As a coach I play not my
eleven best, but my best eleven.*

Knute Rockne[4]

1. Assess the situation
- Has the RD acted in this way on three similar occasions?
- Are you responding disproportionately?
- Did a particular incident trigger the troublesome behaviour?
- Will direct, open discussion relieve the situation?
- Note specific incidents.

2. Stop wishing the RD was different
- Blaming isn't changing.
- Give up believing in fairy tales - they won't magically change!
- Cope with the way they are.

3. Put distance between you and the RD behaviour
- Stand back.
- Identify RD characteristic behaviour.
- What is good/bad with the 'ROUGH' bit of the diamond?
- Separate ball and player.

4. Formulate a plan for interrupting the interaction
- Behaviour is highly interactional.
- What causes the positive cycle? e.g. positive procedure.

5. Implementing the plan

- Timing   - RD not overburdened/stressed.

                          - You have managed time to execute plan effectively.

- Preparation   - Content (what)

                          - Delivery (how)

                          - Location (where)

6. Monitor progress and review process

- Timescale for follow up.

- Identify key factors that will indicate positive change and agree how change will be measured.

Some would suggest that rough diamonds will be sorted out by the team. I don't agree that this can be taken for granted. So I ask myself the following questions and take the appropriate action.

Do the rough bits hurt you?
Your choice.

Do the rough bits hurt the Rough Diamond?
Their choice.

Do the rough bits hurt the team?
No choice.

If the latter they should be treated as C or D players. If C players remain so, they will compromise the outcome of our endeavour. As an immediate judgement call is required to design and deliver an effective performance process for each, this program should have a tight time line. It should not go beyond three 6 week program cycles with detailed monitoring of progress after each 6 week cycle. In my experience the following is most effective. For the first two 6 week cycles, I manage the situation. For the third, just in case it is me who is the problem, I ask another coach/manager to manage. After the 18 weeks, the player is shifted up to B player status, or shifted out of the team. No one should remain a C player beyond 18 weeks.

There can be no soft sentiment in this. We cannot keep those people who lack commitment to being the best that they can be personally; for the team they belong to; and for the badge they represent. Nor can there be lack of commitment and expertise to coach the C player through the 18 weeks. We aim to be in the business of winning persistently, so we cannot consider retaining losers. It is self defeating and hurts the motivational climate we must create for A and B players. If you should consider someone to be a D, admit to an original mistake in their selection but treat as a very tightly and strictly managed C. If they do not move up to C status in 6 weeks move them out. If they do move up, work with them through weeks 7 to 18 as if with a C player.

Persistent Performer Monitoring

This said, selection is seldom a once and for all thing. Often you must think about selection on a day by day basis in sport. Changes in the conditions and circumstances in our arena; wear and tear on our people; thinking ahead to succession; and so on concentrate our minds on having access to back up and the next generation of performers.

So quality selection decisions and continuous monitoring of those selected, and vigilance to identify those who will replace or substitute under performers, the out of form, the injured and the exhausted, are, therefore, essential in creating and monitoring a culture of winning. These decisions are the first priority consequences of the review and in planning for the next challenge. We must develop farther those A and B players and performance manage the C/D players we already have, recruiting where it is necessary on the basis of continuous performer review, to enjoy that culture.

Selection should always be seen as less to do with what people have done, than what they and those selecting believe they can achieve, given our leadership, management, coaching and support, whether that is for a challenge of days, months or years from now. It is the people selected whose performance will determine our results in the next arena and those to follow. We select for the non-negotiable objective of achieving winning results through continuously developing the performance of those we select now and those who will temporarily substitute or replace them in pursuit of winning results. If we fail to select for this objective, it is not only our professional competence that must be questioned, it is our integrity.

Behind the Eyes Lies Attitude

So there must be due diligence exercised in identifying possible attitudes that can emerge in strong existing team members who, given their strengths and status, would be considered automatic choices.

Following a season/campaign/business year:

• Demob happy
These will be older players who see continued selection as playing out their remaining time in anticipation of ending their career. If the team has had a great season, they can slip into cruise mode. If a bad season, they lose confidence

and even commitment. It is important that they are afforded challenge which, after all, is the soul of motivation. They may be given different tasks or roles within the team; they may be challenged to accommodate new team mates and how the team must adjust to them. Whatever, they must face up to the tough reality that there is no personal entitlement to a future. The team comes first.

• Don't change a winning formula
These players want the comfort of the known model of how things are done. They have inertia to exploring new systems even when they are aware that the arena is changing. They must learn to buy into Yogi Berra's notion that *'yesterday's home runs won't win tomorrow's ball games'.* They must actively work at improving on what are, and will become, strengths whilst replacing less effective skills, styles and systems. Their prevailing attitude should be one of constantly seeking to redefine excellence.

• Kismet
They are worrying players because they think that achievement is something that happens rather than something they make happen. It is as if being best on a few occasions means they are excused if it's not every time. There is a sense of fate where they just accept there will be peaks and troughs and if it didn't work this year, by the law of averages, it should be their turn next year. The ethos of winning as *'being better today than they were yesterday'* must be lived. That means constantly seeking how to leverage what they do and how they do it for competitive advantage.

• Fall out
These players get it into their heads that they were the

Yesterday's home runs won't win tomorrow's ball games.

Yogi Berra[5]

Your life is more like a decathlon than a single event. Sometimes you have to work to be better at one event in order to be able to improve in another. And every event helps your total score.

Frank Dick

The ethos of winning as 'being better today than they were yesterday', must be lived.

Frank Dick

There is something much more scarce, something far rarer than ability. It is the ability to recognise ability.

Robert Half[6]

only reason the team was successful; or they were the only good players in an otherwise unsuccessful team without them. As a consequence the natural bonds of teamship are loosened. What doesn't help for them is that new players cannot, in their mind, be up to their standard and so there is a loss of faith in what the team is and means. There is very real need to ensure that the core values of being a team and of being a team member are constantly revisited throughout the duration of a team's life and a team's changes. All members of the team must be recognised, appreciated and rewarded for their quality input.

- **Playing down**
These are the kind of players who believe they and the team are so elevated in standard, that those teams who have less status can be treated with disrespect. They are the ones most likely to see their team eliminated against lesser opposition simply because they played down rather than at their own level. This can even manifest itself in training, 'we've done it, and they haven't – so why push it?' They must learn the discipline of not being seduced by the idea of cruising and resting on laurels. No one is going to lie down and let them win. There are no short cuts to being a winner and remaining so. They must be coached to understand that reducing the rhythm that stretches them in training and in the arena is not an option.

- **Fear of losing**
They are just as prevalent in teams that have won as teams that haven't. It is that low self belief/esteem mindset, which should not be confused with humility or modesty. On the one hand, they are not convinced that they can rise to the challenge again; and on the other, they doubt

they have what it takes to win. The truth is, if the work ethic is executed persistently, there can be no doubts. Accept that there will always be more things to learn and that, when acted upon, they will raise performance. It is only better performance that provides the basis for winning results.

• Old dogs

They are actually really dangerous if they turn their experience into a weapon not only against themselves but new kids on the block. They are reluctant to take on increased levels of training or new ideas. They know best because they have years of experience under their belts. New players are persuaded at every turn to accept their established views. The truth is, they can be gold dust in passing on the benefits of their experience. They are like established artists passing on wisdom to apprentices. This value must be highlighted and developed, while introducing them to the 'new tricks' on what will, hopefully, become a swell of positive motivation in giving them status. This may also be an opportunity to groom next generation coaching or management staff.

Talent programs

Many cynics suggest that selection is quite simply about spotting talent. Talented people, of course, are valuable to the enterprise of creating winners and winning teams. But first, we have to be able to spot talent and that is not easy. According to Robert Half, *'there is something much more scarce, something far rarer than ability. It is the ability to recognise ability.'* There also seems to be some confusion as to what talent is. I believe there are three dimensions.

1. Aptitude

This is a person's suitability to an activity or function. In sport that might be a particular discipline or event or type of sport. Everyone has aptitude for something!

When spotting this, we look at:-

- The status of a person's performance relative to existing basic norms.

- The person's capacities/abilities characteristic of the activity or function.

- The speed of the person's performance improvement.

- The person's performance quality consistency.

When this person adds enjoyment and interest to their aptitude they'll get involved. In sport this is the club level player/athlete.

2. Talented

This is a person whose high level of performance puts them into the territory of competitive excellence. People can only discover how talented they can be once they decide to do something with their aptitude.

When spotting this we look at:-

- The status of a person's performance relative to elite/national/international norms.

- The person's capacities/abilities characteristic of top performers.

- The person's performance stability and excellence under competitive pressure and in adversity.

When this person adds high work capacity and will to win to their talent, they'll commit to winning persistently. In sport, they are your national team.

3. Genius

This is a person whose performance excellence puts them in a class apart. They are excitingly and often uncomfortably unique. Spotting them is not easy because for the most part we are not sure what we are looking for, though we certainly know when we have found it!

- The status of the person's performance is beyond existing norms. It is not only better, it is different.

- The person's capacities/abilities exceed and/or are different from what is considered to be world class.

- The genius can and will persistently raise their game to out perform whatever the opposition offers or however adverse the situation.

- They reinvent excellence; redefine performance.

- They see things differently and make a difference with what they see.

When this person adds work capacity and passion to their genius they go beyond winning to invent new parameters of excellence. In sport, they are the stuff of legends who we may be fortunate enough to see once in a generation. When spotted and recruited they will develop and deliver only given the specific coaching, management and leadership they need.

Whether selected for their aptitude or for being talented or as a genius, each person represents a specific set of coaching challenges. So make sure that you are equally careful when selecting coaches. One final thought on selection, and in particular, talent spotting from 'Winning'.[7]

> 'To spot a winning athlete, I am convinced
> you must look first and foremost for athletes
> with passion to achieve the best in their
> chosen arena .... Talent always comes
> a poor second.'

Considerable talent will be in each person you look to select, but they do not have to be the most talented. The passion to win will overcome the shortfall. I have not changed my mind in that.

Chapter 7

TEAMSHIP

None of us is as good as all of us, provided we each share a responsibility to help get the best out of each other together. That means persistently bringing personal role excellence to the team endeavours. It also means understanding the role of everyone else in the team to give the right assistance, support or pass at the right moment. The shared sense of purpose is founded on shared values.

Teams and Teamwork

I believe the problem with words like 'team' and 'teamwork' is that, because they are in frequent common usage, we all understand their meaning. But I am not too sure about that. When each of us is driving towards our goal and we see someone better placed than we are to deliver for the team, do we intuitively bring them into the game to support or take over? When we see someone in the team struggling because they have a problem, do we intuitively give them the support they need or take the pressure off them?

The real value of a team is its strength through interdependence and this is something for which we are each actively responsible. We don't decide to pass the ball because we have run out of ideas but because we see the advantage that the pass will bring to the team.

When someone in the team has a problem, it is not their problem it is the team's. No one tries to under perform for the team, nor do they try to get things wrong - unless I am mistaken. I can't imagine someone looking into the mirror in the morning and declaring 'today I'm going to screw up!' No, people are trying to do the right thing for the team. So if they are in trouble and we know how to help them out yet do nothing, what sort of team are we? So what is teamwork? According to Ian McGeechan:

> *'The team is different from a collection of individuals in that it has a common purpose; that it has an understanding, collectively, of what it is trying to achieve.'*

This explains the concept of what a team is more accurately than Michael Caine in The Italian Job (1969):

> *'....we'll get through it, if we work as a team and that means you do everything I say!'*

The team shares an understanding of why it is going into the arena and what must be done to win. Delivering on that is teamwork.

Team Skills

How that is achieved comes down to three broad sets of skills:

- The number on the shirt (ROLE)
- The badge on the front of the shirt (TEAM)
- The name on the back of the shirt (YOU)

When you pass the ball, you don't give away responsibility, you accept it.

Ian McGeechan[1]

You have to know how a player likes to receive the ball. We don't all like to receive the ball the same way.

Andy Roxburgh[2]

It doesn't matter who scores the points, it's who can get the ball to the scorer.

Larry Bird[3]

The pass has to be one that the player can use. If he can't use it, you've given it away.

Johan Cruyff[4]

Team players play for the badge on the front, not the name on the back!

The Number on the Shirt

This is the performer's role or position in the team; their technical strengths, their specialism. So the person is selected for excellence in terms of their role in contributing to the sports team, business team, military team, science or medical team, orchestra and so on. It is for such excellence that the person is developed farther to contribute to a winning outcome for the team.

Role excellence on the one hand relates to delivering personal performance quality which is the meat of Chapter 10. If there is a number 6 on the shirt, the player aims to be the greatest number 6 in every respect. The player certainly aims to be better than the opposition number 6 and in holding advantage in any engagement or challenge by the opposition. That challenge often comes down to one person. This represents an on-going dual in the arena where the result is determined by coming out on top. All players in a team must be aware of that and contribute to the team effort accordingly.

In the 2005 UEFA Champions League, most people will remember that the hero in the end for Liverpool v AC Milan, was goalkeeper Jerzy Dudek. And in my opinion that was actually the outcome of a dual that had been going on throughout the game between Dudek and Andrei Shevchenko. Liverpool were 3-0 down at half time. In the 52nd minute Shevchenko swerved a free kick round the Liverpool wall and Dudek dived to make an incredible save when a goal seemed certain. The goal would have sealed Liverpool's fate. Shevchenko shook his head in disbelief.

Extra time was played because Liverpool tied the game at 3–3. After 27 minutes of extra time, a cross from the left found Shevchenko unmarked 8 metres in front of the goal with only Dudek to beat. He headed for goal; Dudek stopped it but the ball rebounded to Shevchenko's feet. He struck a perfect shot, Dudek deflected it over the bar. Shevchenko held his face in his hands. The saves had seemed impossible. Dudek had now denied him three times. So, imagine the difference between Dudek's and Shevchenko's self belief when Dudek handed the ball to Shevchenko for his penalty. Their faces said everything at that moment. Dudek saved again. Each moment of the dual brought it to this conclusion. The victory was Dudek's. The championship was Liverpool's.

The performer's role, the number on the shirt, has special significance in competitions where contribution involves recording a personal score or result and adding it to that of colleagues, representing the team score. Ryder Cup and Davis Cup singles and the European Cup in athletics are examples in sport. Sales figures are an example in business. These are pretty obvious because they come down to clear measures and numbers. Where things are less obvious, are areas such as support and facilitation roles.

Common sense suggests that in any organisation each role is there to serve an essential purpose or they would not be there. Those who achieve the measures and numbers can only achieve them if they have been put in a position to do so by those who facilitate or support. The outcome of any team endeavour is the consequence of what and how people have delivered through their roles. It is like a series of cogged wheels in a machine. Each must function perfectly or the machine cannot be effective. Failure of one role compromises the outcome. Each person in each role must understand the value they represent; must be afforded the preparation and training to deliver that value; and must deliver. This is about every single person in the team pulling their weight and in doing so knowing a genuine sense of responsibility for, and pride in, the team's achievement.

This is why it is so important for everyone in a business to understand the 'customer's experience' and the 'customer's journey'. The former is the experienced reality of every point of contact the customer has with the business and it is evaluated by the customer. The latter is the pathway of points of contact the customer will encounter in purchasing the service or product offering and in enjoying after sales service. It is evaluated by the business and to be honest, there are normally a lot more points than most people think. Of course there is the initial greeting and service in a store, or showroom; a hospital or in a hotel or restaurant. But there is also how someone hears about the business, an enquiry telephone call, a comment reflecting someone else's experience; the delivery of a service or product; how a problem was handled; after sales follow up and support. And there are many more!

Each point of contact involves someone delivering their role in the process. It is essential that the person doing so is excellent in that role and understands where it sits in the process. Great customer experience at every point means both customer and business win. Poor performance at any point and no-one wins – except another business the customer now heads for! Think of it this way, if someone took a photograph of you at any moment in your competitive arenas in life, would you always be proud to put your autograph on it and say 'this is me at my best'?

The Badge on the Front of the Shirt

The badge skills are about connectedness, communication, cohesion, co-operation and consideration. Here, each of us must understand we are all interdependent and that, in being so, we are individually and collectively, stronger. We use our own genius to get the best out of others and their genius to get the best out of ourselves.

I think I only really began to understand this aspect of teamwork when the concept of passing the ball was explained to me. This does not happen in track and field athletics! Ronaldinho[5] describes it thus:

> 'My role in the team is to create plays, to provide the last pass before a goal is scored. To assist: this is my role. To put a team-mate in a position to score. That is my biggest concern. When I train, one of the things I concentrate on is creating a mental picture of how best to deliver that ball to a team-mate preferably leaving him alone in front of the rival goalkeeper. So what I do, always, before a game, every night and every day, is try and think up things, imagine plays, which no one else will have thought of, and to do so always bearing in mind the particular strengths of each team-mate to whom I am passing the ball. When I construct those plays in my mind I take into account whether one team-mate likes to receive the ball at his feet, or ahead of him; if he is good with his head, and how he prefers to head, whether he is stronger on his right or left, that is my job. That is what I do.'

On reflection, those words not only describe teamwork, they are indicative of great leadership. So the quality of the pass and the decision to make it are pretty important. Like assisting, supporting and communication, they are essential to constructive connectedness. They all really matter. These things, when done well, should be valued. They should be recognised, appreciated and rewarded. If you consistently give perfect passes for other people to score yet they ignore you while bathing in the crowd's adulation, do you feel highly motivated to continue that service? I think not. Those thoughts, actions and behaviours we value and see excellently executed we should demonstrably appreciate – or they may not become the norm.

But let's take this a step farther. When it comes to the point of passing the ball, the receiver might be thought of as a customer. They in turn, will have a customer. If we are to give the customer the perfect pass needed, we also need to know the pass that the customer's customer needs. In fact, when we get this picture right, the customer's customer will coach us on the right ball to give the customer! So, the way I see the concept is not to pass the ball to the customer, it is to pass it through the customer. In passing, assisting, supporting or facilitating we must be aware of what will happen next or at least what options the receiver will have. This concept of connectedness is a winning difference when persistently delivered in practice.

The Name on the back of the Shirt: 'You'

The third set of skills is all about the unique personal qualities that someone brings to the team, the *chemistry* in the selection criteria (see page 95). This is the unique difference that makes the difference. In a team, collective achievement comes down to managing the diversity whilst leveraging its strength.

The real power of teamwork, then, is to effect synergies that combine to maximise the influence of individual strengths and to reduce the influence of individual shortcomings on the collective endeavour. The point to remember here is that people are selected for the team because of their strengths. These will be in the context of their number and badge skills, naturally, but there will also be something that comes with the 'you' skills. All of these strengths in bringing a special value to the team, set them apart. So it is these that must have priority in their continuous development. They may be physical, mental or emotional strengths and will contribute progressively to the unique shape of the team. I also believe that, for example, the drive and ability to grow towards leadership and related roles rest in the 'you' skills.

Figure 9

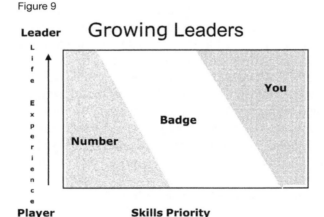

The priority of these three broad sets of skills has a changing profile as people learn through their life experiences. Great teams will attract and grow great individuals who, in certain contexts, are 'stars'. But being a star cannot become the focus of all that is negative about inflated 'egos'. John Wooden[6] put this in context: *'The main ingredient of stardom is the rest of the team.'*

Initially, it is mostly the **Number** skills that have priority and less of the **You** skills. Ultimately that priority is reversed. The **Badge** skills, however, remain consistent in their value throughout (figure 9). Of course, if everyone in the team worked only on how to make themselves even more different than the others, the outcome would be chaos! This is where quality of team leadership comes into its own. The strength of the team rests with the strength of the leader to harmonise inputs to a perfect whole.

Cohesion

There's a useful acronym to help get the Number, Badge and You skills right in practice:

> **J**oin up the dots
> **A**lign everything with vision and values
> **M**anage relationships

• Join up the dots

This is about seeing the world we are in as if we are in the centre of a sphere with eyes that can see in every direction. The customer's customer concept reflects this. And it is more than connecting people. It is seeking the connections between ideas, objects, people, the familiar and the unfamiliar to gain advantage for the team. It is joining up the dots of all three **JAM** headings. It is connecting what you and others in the team could do differently individually or collectively, or what different things can be done to achieve advantage. It is developing action phrases instead of action words. It is stretching then connecting the physical, the mental and the emotional. Out of this grows a flexibility at personal level that gives game plan versatility at team level. It is testing assumptions, asking 'why not?' and imagining new ways of doing things. It is opening up to different approaches to tactics, training, combinations of players, leadership styles, team line-ups and game plans.

• Alignment

Here is where everyone must act on the responsibility of their commitment to making the journey necessary to achieving the vision, while living the team's shared values. People must go beyond the edge of risk in facing the challenge of flexibility in what they do and how they do it. They must become comfortable with the unfamiliar and be willing to go the distance to become excellent in its delivery. That includes learning about themselves and the opposition. And for coaches and managers who provide overall leadership direction they must honour the ownership message in ways that in former times were off limits. So, for example, team members should be invited to offer their own team selections for consideration and be encouraged to defend such, as what is best for the team. They must be challenged to come up with ideas and game plans and on leadership decisions. They should also be challenged to define the quality they will aspire to and commit to climbing the mountain to get there.

Sometimes in business this can seem a step too far. But is it? Often near enough is felt to be good enough. Businesses can return impressive profits and continue to grow without even being close to being the best. But how does this align with the stretching of vision and strong values most would proudly proclaim? Surely if everyone in a business understood what alignment is and were committed to being the best personally and as a business, their surge in performance would make them want to keep going till, as a team, they *are* the best.

The economic catastrophe in the winter of 2008 /2009 clearly exposed those who did not think this way. They thought, acted and behaved in an 'I will survive' channel and underlined the weakness of such an attitude in arenas that will become far tougher and more competitive in the years to follow. Alignment in business is essential if it is to shift to an 'I will win' channel.

• Managing Relationships

There is not one relationship in our lives that does not benefit from working on it. Understanding that everyone we enjoy a relationship with matters is fundamental to social cohesion. So everyone in the team matters, every relationship in the team matters. It is essential that we know everyone in our team and what they do. Alex Ferguson suggests, *'the essence of teamwork is that everyone understands the role of each other'.* That goes beyond the players to both technical and non-technical staff in the organisation. From chief executives to cleaners, all are essential parts of the team and must be valued as such by everyone in the team. They are neither bosses nor servants. Each is as responsible for the team's and organisation's success or shortcomings as players or workforce. Relationships must reflect the mutual respect that this suggests. People throughout the team earn respect for their commitment to the team and for the excellence with which they deliver their role.

I honestly believe that getting this right brings a proper sense of consideration for others that extends beyond the moments of fighting for advantage in the arena. I consider this to be critical because it reinforces the instinct to connect in the arena.

When I was advising on fitness with West Hartlepool

The essence of teamwork is that everyone understands the role of each other.

Alex Ferguson[7]

Am I not destroying my enemies when I make friends of them.

Abraham Lincoln[8]

The strength of the pack is the wolf, and the strength of the wolf is the pack.

Rudyard Kipling[9]

Snowflakes are one of nature's most fragile things, but just look at what they can do when they stick together.

Anon

Rugby Club, a training camp was held at Loughborough University Campus. At the end of the first full training day, Barry Taylor, the coach, announced arrangements for dinner and most of the team disappeared towards the hotel. Behind them they left empty plastic water bottles, torn-off strappings, various discarded wrappings and so on. Barry took a black bin bag and we began tidying up the field. Rob Wainwright who was to captain Scotland, and Derek Patterson, Scottish scrum half, moved at speed to gather in the litter – then took the bin bag to the rubbish bin. Nothing was said by Barry nor by me. Yet the next evening all players involved themselves in the same tidying up operation and it became normal not only during the camp but when leaving changing rooms after practice and games.

At Ipswich Town Academy, it became routine after practice for players to fill another couple of plastic cups with water in addition to their own and pass the extra cups on to team-mates who were slower due to fatigue to get back to the water fountain.

The outcome of the Rolls Royce Renaissance program substantially improved an aspect of production by simply applying the old dictum 'leave things as you'd expect to find them'. That's an old fashioned value but it scores high in respect and consideration. Over time, the end of one shift in a factory saw the workplace left with ample evidence of the kind of residual mess that let you know the site had seen some serious action! The incoming shift then had to clean up the mess, taking up very unproductive time, before they could get started. There was little motivation, then, for them to leave the area other than they'd found it! Through the Renaissance program, the shift teams developed tidier working practices, leaving things in pristine condition for the next shift which, in turn, became normal behaviour. It was almost a competition in itself to see who could leave the area cleanest! The impact on energies, efficiency, safety and motivation was huge. This consideration thing really works! Maybe all it needs is practicing behavioural change.

Managing relationships effectively does not necessarily mean that everyone in a team will be the very best of friends. Rather, it is about ensuring that there are no tensions in the professional or team or organisational relationships that will compromise the endeavour. Any such tension must be addressed and resolved before attitudes have a chance to polarise. Mutual respect, appreciation and trust do not require close personal friendship. One final thought on consideration. The foundation of mutual respect has been extended in many sports teams to adopt the principle that since the load is shared in training and in competition – the rewards should likewise be shared – equally.

Values

And what of team values, those that enrich the special bond which defines the team and will have every member carry for life an indelible memory of closeness? There are many admirable values which organisations will proudly make their own, having taken time to involve all staff in identifying and stating them. Most capture the spirit of the following list:

Honesty of endeavour from preparation and training to every moment in the arena. In every relationship from senior leadership and management, to support staff, to work teams, this certainly keeps people aligned in the team. In my experience it creates a climate where there are no unpleasant surprises and a culture where the messenger is not shot for getting bad news to those who must hear it! Honesty may be perceived as something that exists between people. But in truth, it exists only when you are honest with yourself.

Integrity is about living the team's shared values in thought, behaviour and action. On occasion an individual may suggest their personal integrity has been threatened by some event involving the team. If this is the perception, then, clearly, the team's values are not shared by that person. It is right that every individual reflects candour in stating how he or she feels, and there should be opportunity to do so openly, or there will be a growing sense of disengagement within the team. But in all of this, part of personal integrity relates unequivocally to putting the team's pursuit of purpose above personal sensitivities. To be honest, integrity is one of these values that should be a given in any organisation but it is still worth stating. 'Real integrity' according to Oprah Winfrey[10], 'is doing the right thing, knowing that nobody's going to know whether *you* did it or not.'

Trust always goes in at least two directions. When I coach you to take ownership in the arena, I trust you to do the right thing out there to deliver the performance of your life. And you trust me to have prepared you correctly. Then, whatever has happened in the arena when you step from it, you trust me to do the right thing to help you learn from the experience and I trust you to be honest in your self appraisal and to practice what is learned so that you are even better next time. When it comes to a team-mate and trust, in their eyes you will see someone who will be the wind beneath your wings when you need them to be because they know you will do the same for them. That is trust. Some people think the process starts with *earning* trust so that they are perceived as trustworthy. I don't agree. It starts with *giving* trust so that they are perceived as being trusting.

Loyalty is something that has had to be refocused in its sense. A realistic picture of loyalty to the organisation and to the individual has less to do with contract than with mutual commitment and trust. There was a time when joining a team or an organisation was the start of a life-long relationship. For some that remains the situation, but if other organisations were armies, the ratio of regular soldiers to mercenaries has changed over time!

In these organisations, employers naturally expect loyalty from all in the organisation. 'Regular soldiers' (those who wish a life-long relationship with the organisation) see loyalty as reflected in that. The 'mercenaries' (those who give 100% to the organisation for some years – then move on) see loyalty as important of course but as something that is transferable. These different views of loyalty must be reconciled if there is to be team cohesion in pursuit of a common purpose. Leadership must be mindful of this.

I believe that mutual loyalty comes from organisations growing a climate where the people feel *'this is the organisation I want to give my all for'*; and the organisation feels *'no people punch their weight more effectively than ours'*. That means the organisation fully and persistently delivering on commitment to giving each person the right level of challenge to realise their aspirations. It also means each person fully and persistently delivering on commitment to be the winning difference for the organisation. In other words, loyalty must not be assumed. It must be worked for. Given the strength of that loyalty, it will bind to the organisation those who commit their working life to it. And, should people move on, or organisations have to release people, the organisation grows a reputation which attracts only the best people; and for giving its people the best preparation for whatever challenges they will face at work and in life. This theme is visited again in Chapter 12.

Communication is as essential a connective tissue to the team as blood is to the body. It must be a constant movement by movement dynamic enhancing effectiveness of the team by enhancing effectiveness of the individuals. In team sport, in the competitive arena, it has immense value in keeping team-mates informed about where advantage can be gained or where there are threats. It also enriches the motivational climate and makes it possible to learn, adapt and change with agility.

So, when in the competitive arena, players must keep talking to each other. On a day to day basis this can become diluted when it is assumed or when other events seem to deserve priority. That's why, in every organisation, it is important to formalise regular communication 'pit stops'. This ensures key messages don't miss their mark. Sloppy communication can too often create situations where the target is hit but the point is missed. If that happens it can cause confusion and inefficiency on the one hand and offence on the other. Two important points about communication:-

- Always check that the message received is the one intended. Normally, that's confirmed by the receiver translating the message into the effective action that the sender intended.

- Make sure that the medium is the best means of communication in a given situation. We have four areas of choice in this:

- Electronic - email, text.
- Personal - face to face, teleconferencing
- Oral - presentation, podcast, telephone, CD.
- Written - printed material, faxes, hard copy etc.

So, for example, general information for quick updates is suited to email, but a personal performance de-brief is not! Blackberries score low on emotional intelligence! There are painful consequences for all concerned in breaking faith with values – so keep the faith!

Stars

Occasionally, there will be players who have ability that puts them in a class apart compared with other players in the team. Because of this, they will attract more attention than the other players. This is only dangerous if not managed sensibly and sensitively.

This is where the truly great player in a team learns that character is something you have, not something you are. Being part of a team means you cease to exist as an individual when you pull on the shirt for practice or for a match. At that point the player's purpose is team greatness. It is also where the player learns that to remain great, he or she must work even harder than those who don't quite match their ability. That means in training, as demonstrated by Daley Thompson training on Christmas Day. He knew his rivals would not! It also means doing so when playing for the team, as David Beckham did for England in that extraordinary game against Greece at Old Trafford in 2002. He worked himself to exhaustion and still managed to score the winning goal. Very early the attitude 'I can do the job when I turn it on' evaporates because the player turns it on from the moment the game starts. Every great performer has admitted to learning some hard lessons in this respect.

Team Build and Quality Consistency

The process of building a team has the same five steps for the team as a whole and for fitting individual players into the team. This applies as much to building the leadership team and the support infrastructure, as to the players or work teams or departments, etc.

1. Select   This has already been discussed in some detail in Chapter 3. It is about selecting the best team which is not necessarily the same as selecting the best players.

2. Develop   This has been the focus of Chapters 6 and 7.

3. Involve   This is really an extension of development where players have learned to take the lead in their own growth within the team and of the growth of the team itself. Chapter 1 also has relevance here.

4. Inspire   Creating the right motivational climate enriches their motivation to be who they must be. Chapter 11 helps give this focus.

5. Unleash   Ownership of their individual performance and that of the team is theirs, individually. Chapter 10 fits with this.

Team performance excellence is something that must be delivered today whilst establishing the basis for a team excellence dynasty. We want to have a team that will always challenge for the win. Obviously that will not

Build for your team a feeling of oneness, of dependence on one another and of strength to be derived by unity.

Vince Lombardi[11]

Talent wins games, but teamwork and intelligence wins championships.

Michael Jordan[12]

Individually we are one drop. Together we are an ocean.

Ryunosuke Satoro[13]

always involve the same people. In sport, players may be injured, lose form, be fatigued, move clubs, come to the end of their career, get suspended. In business people are promoted, get sick, move departments, move to another business, are casualties in downsizing, come to the end of their career. So other people must take their place. When that happens, neither the person coming into the team nor the team as a whole must feel that they are less of a 'first team performer' than the person they replace or the previous team. Everyone in the team is responsible for delivering team excellence which means that everyone must believe that they and their team mates are the best people for the roles they have in the team.

So there must be a strategy for growing people into 'first team' roles through progressive awareness of the role and of experience in it. In sport that can be watching from the bench, coming off the bench or playing in low key occasions. It can also be in operating some kind of rotation policy. I believe that a similar strategy and adoption of rotation policy should be applied in business. This will ensure that we responsibly address the 'Form' and 'Forward' criteria of the 6 F's in Chapter 6.

If such a strategy does not become normal in both sport and business, the team and organisation become extremely vulnerable. For example, if there is no sense of varying pressure across a team so that not all people are at maximum stretch over months, then all will fatigue at the same time! Under the heading of 'Forward' criteria, the team all pass their 'sell by' date at the same time. There must be a staggered cycle across the team of peak performance periods: of learning, developing and retraining; and of regeneration. This ensures consistent high quality team performance. It is worth bearing in mind, in this context, that at the end of the quarterly campaign or business year everyone is working flat out to achieve targets. Yet the very next day after that period ends the next campaign begins. That's a pretty tough challenge if everyone has worked themselves into the ground! A 'momentum maintenance' program should ensure performance quality consistency (see page 176).

We recognise not everyone in every team will play the perfect game every time the team is out there (see 'Form' page 97) but between them they must produce a performance which returns the right team results. It is essential that a strategy is in place to ensure that the preparation of players and team delivers on this through quality consistency.

Finally, as Dan Topolski[14] points out, it is also important that there is a strategy in place for newcomers to the team. I agree with Dan's opinion on this.

> *'Introducing a new member into the team or new members into the team can be difficult. The coach can help a lot by briefing the team about the person coming in; making sure that the person coming in understands what the team is. But in the end, that person has got to make his or her own way and earn their place in the team.'*

Pulling your Weight

To summarise this chapter, I'd like to use the Oxford – Cambridge Boat Race (figure 10), and, in particular, the 2003 event. Cambridge had come into the race out and out favourites to win. But Oxford did not see it that way. If they could put in a performance that gave them a lead at Barnes Bridge (position 13 in figure 10) they may just be able to hold off the powerful Cambridge finish. The race normally lasts around 17 to 18 minutes. There are eight oarsmen in the boat and each will put the blade of their oar into the water roughly 600 times during the race. The cox is the only person in the boat who can actually see where they are going! How about that for trusting the leader!

Each time they pull the blade through the water is their unique contribution to the boat's progress. It is the most

Figure 10

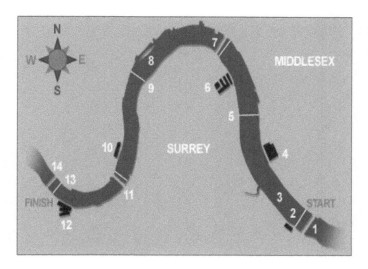

physically exhausting of sports and the Thames race holds extremely tough challenges. Some oarsmen might think 'Well there are another seven guys in my boat – I'll pull really hard for 550 and they can carry me for the other 50' – 'or maybe they can help me out for 10'. But that's not how it is for a team player.

The race was won by Oxford by 20cm (8 inches). If an oarsman had not pulled his weight – even for one stroke, and they had lost by 20cm, he'd know where that 20cm had been lost. Teams win because each person in the team pulls their weight 100% every time and because they know their team-mates are doing the same. That way, working together, each player knows they made the winning difference.

Chapter 8

COACHWORKS

Our job as coaches is done when those we coach are no longer dependent on our guidance. They own each moment in their arenas and responsibly accept self management, regulation and motivation in all things: their judgement calls in making decisions persistently hit the mark: they intuitively raise the bar in delivering personal performance excellence. We get there by progressively shifting the nature of our coaching role from being the light to standing out of the light, and by our vigilance in raising the bar that measures our effectiveness as coaches.

Coaches and Coaching

Coaches help people perform better through a piece of timely advice or through years of influencing a person's development. Many people coach intuitively and are unaware that they do. We can each recall someone who, on reflection, coached us to make better progress than we would have on our own to reach where we are now. Coaches invest expertise, energy and time in people. That's why I've always thought that organisations who earn the coveted 'Investors in People' award, have achieved their coaching qualification! The concept of investment reflects a very particular mindset as set out in an essay by Ralph Waldo Emerson.[1]

> *'In the order of nature, we cannot render benefits to those from whom we receive them, or only seldom, but the benefit we receive must be rendered again, line by line, deed for deed, cent for cent to somebody.'*

In other words, we can't always 'pay it back' to our parents, our teachers, our coaches, our managers, our friends, indeed to anyone who has helped us on our way. So we have to 'pay it forward' just as they did for us. They raised us to stand on their shoulders; we must raise those who follow on to ours.

Great coaches across the range of sports live this concept. In the movie 'Pay it Forward', schoolboy Trevor came up with the idea of 'paying it forward' to three other people. Each of them would do likewise and so on. This was Trevor's response to the challenge made by his teacher to 'think of an idea to change our world and put it into action'.

I believe coaches change the world by changing people, by helping raise their performance. In sport, coaches not only prepare people for sport but also through sport, for life. The lessons you learn in training to achieve better performance apply in equal measure to how you can live a better life. That surely is the very strong message proposed by John Wooden[2] in his 'Pyramid of Success' (figure 11). The coaching process helps athletes on their journey to be the best that they can be. The coach cannot do it for them. The coach cannot put in what is not there already. There is a story about Michelangelo which I think sums up the situation. It is said he was asked 'how could you create something as beautiful as the statue of David from an ugly block of marble?' He evidently replied 'the beauty was always there. It was my job to get rid of the bits that were not'. The outcome of the coaching

Figure 11

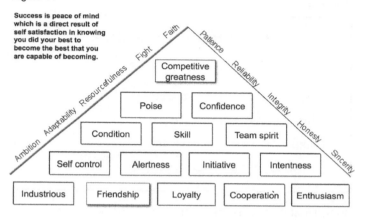

Success is peace of mind which is a direct result of self satisfaction in knowing you did your best to become the best that you are capable of becoming.

Adapted from John Wooden

process is to prepare the person being coached to deliver personal excellence and to continuously pursue farther development: to **O**wn, **D**ecide, **D**o!

The Coaching Process

The way I see it is this. There are four broad phases to the process as the coach prepares the athlete (figure 12).

1. The coach is the light that lights the athlete's way. This is when athletes need a carefully prescribed program enabling them safely to learn and practice their skills and role effectively. It is about establishing a strong foundation and a winning attitude. Here the athlete is *learning to learn.*

2. The coach teaches athletes to generate their own light. They are helped to understand that mistakes are learning opportunities. It is through such learning and reinforcement of the increasing number of elements working for them that they will develop and grow. The coach still leads, building

Figure 12

COACHING PROCESS

BE THE LIGHT.....................(DIRECT)
FUEL THE LIGHT.....................(COACH)

ROOTS TO GROW

REFLECT THE LIGHT ....(SUPPORT)
STAND OUT OF THE LIGHT...(COUNSEL)

WINGS TO FLY

on the first phase. There is, however, a growing sense that process is being fuelled by the athletes' winning attitude. Here the athlete is *learning to perform*.

3. The coach becomes a mirror for the athlete's light. The athlete is taking more control as both coach and athlete challenge each other as the athlete takes control. As the athlete grows through this process, the coach exercises judgement in managing the dynamics of a tension between challenge and support. That tension can be likened to a tightrope along which the athlete must travel

Figure 13

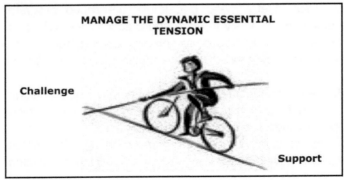

MANAGE THE DYNAMIC ESSENTIAL TENSION

Challenge

Support

(figure 13). Initially, there is more support than challenge, but this will change as the athlete progresses. Too much support and the athlete is ill prepared for challenges of ownership: too much challenge and the athlete may break down. The coach must take time to learn how to read the athlete's needs to get these judgement calls right. Here, the athlete is *performing to learn.*

4. The coach stands out of the light as the athlete takes full ownership of their journey. The coach is always there to be the wind beneath their wings when that is needed. It is the athlete who decides when it is needed. Here the athlete is *performing to win.*

This process applies in developing the athlete's range of skills from technical to behavioural and for whatever role. It also applies in growing the team from a group of high performing individual parts to a cohesive, excellence – delivering whole.

Coaching Systems

Coaches must know what they know; they must know what they don't know; and they must know who does! There are three systems that can be applied in coaching. There is the *transfer* where the athlete passes from one coach to another, each specialising in a stage of development. This is like going from teacher to teacher as you progress through school years. Then there is the *escort* where the coach takes you through the whole journey from being a beginner to being an elite performer. Finally, there is the *partnership* where there are several coaching or performance related inputs which change as the athlete progresses along the development journey and the coach's competence to lead the progression is tested.

No coach can know everything. Often the person being coached may even be ahead of the coach in some areas of competence. When this is clear, it rests with both coach and the person being coached to introduce people with more advanced knowledge. What cannot happen is that the athlete becomes victim of the coach's limitations. And we all have these! It is generally agreed that the process is athlete centred, coach led and performance related services supported. This is actually the partnership system in practice as shown in figure 14. Within the performance related services there are many additional specialist coaching inputs, sport and medical science and so on.

Figure 14

TEAM COACH - ATHLETE/TEAM

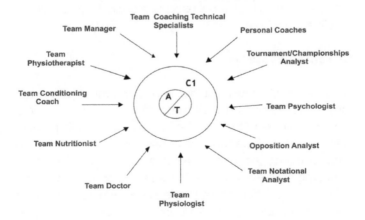

These services represent areas of information that may influence the coach's decision making in guiding the athlete's or team's performance, development and delivery. The process might be represented by figure 14a. The outer

Figure 14a

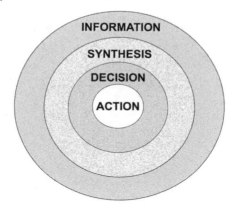

ring of information and intelligence is synthesised to a form which the coach understands as relevant to the decision that must be made. This, in turn, translates to effective action by athlete or team. The journey of the process is from the outer ring to the centre.

For the most part, in business and in sport, it is the coach who undertakes the synthesis in addition to the decision making. Education and experience must prepare the coach for this. At the elite performance level, however, input of information and intelligence, especially from the sciences, has become extremely sophisticated and complex to the point where it is unreasonable to expect coaches to perform the essential level of synthesis in order to make the right decisions and apply those decisions to the advantage of athlete and team. These decisions can affect the millimetres or milliseconds that separate victory from defeat.

So in an increasing number of sports at the elite performance level a Performance Director, Performance Services Manager or similar role has been created to organise and co-ordinate the services, then synthesise the information this represents for the coach. The coach

Figure 14b

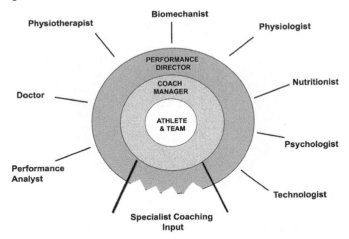

then has higher probability of making the right decisions and judgement calls. Practically, the process might be illustrated as in figure 14b.

Figure 15

APPLYING THE COACHING MODEL TO YOU

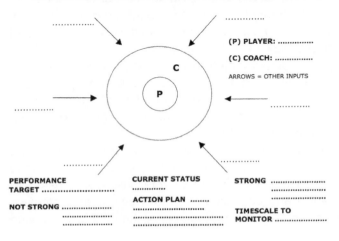

I believe we each can apply a similar coaching model to ourselves. Figure 15 keeps it simple. If you are in the centre of the model, who is the coach and what other inputs do you need to build two or three of your strengths and address two or three of those areas where you are not so strong? Coach and athlete work together to design the athlete's development and performance plan, applying the **GROWL** model or a variant of it (see Chapter 9). After six weeks there is a progress review where the athlete's progress, plan appropriateness and coach effectiveness are reviewed. This is not a judgemental occasion, it is a learning occasion.

Some years ago I was working with Jeanie Bergin, a creative thinking expert and colleague from the USA. I'd got really mad at an athlete who I thought had really messed up. She said *'Frank, your problem is that you think the opposite of right is wrong. It's not, it's left! The athlete's just lost direction'*. Reviews let you see whether coach and/or plan and/or athlete are on or off track. If off track, it's all about learning fast how to get back on track again. Sounding off about things won't get people back on track. Learning fast, and doing something about it, will. Review information is referred to the performance database and leads to a prescription for change. Then, the development process continues in its cyclical **OPERA** progression described on page 177. Each cycle builds on the next in pursuit of the annual goal and the eventual long term goal of the athlete to be the very best that he/she can be.

Key Coach Competencies

There are five broad areas of competency which the effective coach must develop:-

• Technical knowledge
The coach must have the technical knowledge,

experience and expertise necessary to addressing the athlete's coaching needs. If the athlete is being coached in speed skating, then the coach must have the relevant technical knowledge. It is not necessary for the coach to have been an elite performer personally but must have deep understanding of all technical aspects – techniques, training and tactical. In most instances, the coach will, however, have some practical experience of personal technical development and performance in a competitive arena.

It is relatively seldom that great sports performers become great coaches. In football, for example, while Franz Beckenbauer and Johan Cruyff went on to become great coaches, Alex Ferguson and Arsene Wenger did not really achieve the level of greatness as players which they enjoy as managers. Technical knowledge is secured through study and being vigilant in always being up to date with technical developments. Learning through practical experience is built on that platform.

• Coaching method
The coach must have understanding of the skills, styles, systems and process of coaching, and expertise in their application in practice. It is an advantage to have been on the receiving end of coaching, to help understand where emotional intelligence and, in particular, empathy, fits within the coach-athlete relationship. The best coaches have an insatiable hunger for their personal growth. They not only seek nourishment from their own sport but from anywhere highest quality effective coaching is evident. Coaches in sport learn as much from coaching in business, from the performing arts and from other professions, as they do from sport.

While in sport there are coach education and certification programs offered from local to international level, in business there has been a steady increase in the quality and quantity of programs to diploma and degree level via colleges and universities. They are undoubtedly excellent in affording a wealth of knowledge in the relevant sciences, probably leaning more towards counselling and mentoring rather than the traditional picture of coaching. This, however, brings deeper understanding of the behavioural change processes involved in developing people for their chosen arenas in life.

Of course, coaches learn about coaching methods through study of relevant literature, participating in conferences, attending courses in pursuit of qualifications and so on. These afford the coach, counsellor or mentor a most valuable foundation. However, in my experience this is very seldom enough, because whatever title we give to the leader of the overall change process, their's is a practical art which must produce practical outcomes in the shape of better and/or different performance which leads to improved results. This is how coaches are measured in sport. The same should apply to all coaching. I have known coaches whose academic knowledge is breathtaking but who simply don't deliver in practice.

So, on that foundation, the coach must build carefully monitored, guided or mentored experience. The coach must also look to studying, shadowing and working with experienced effective coaches. There can be little doubt that, in time, you create your own 'brand' of coaching but that is the outcome of years of practical coaching. I guess that is the same for mentoring and counselling. Whatever shape your 'brand' takes, it is essential to bear in mind that its style cannot become more significant or memorable than the lesson or message. Delivering the message aggressively is probably more to do with the coach's frustration than the choice of style! It may be effective on a couple of occasions but it should not become a reputation, or the messages can eventually mean little.

When people call you 'coach' it reflects a very special kind of respect, because they believe you will enrich their lives by helping them achieve far more than they would on their own, or with someone else. When you coach people you acknowledge a very special kind of responsibility to do and be what you must, to reward the trust they have in you. Your delivery on commitment to continuous learning and persistent growth as a coach, and of applying that to the athlete's advantage, earns that respect, and equips you to fully execute that responsibility.

• Syntheses of inputs

Immense strides have been made in turning awareness that performance development can be influenced by a multitude of variables into accessing intelligence on those relevant to the athlete being coached, then acting effectively on that intelligence to the athlete's advantage. In sport, these variables may belong to the realm of psychology, physiology, nutrition, bio-mechanics, lifestyle management, medicine, performance factor analysis and so on; or to specialist technical coaching or fitness training, etc. Whether a coach is coaching an individual athlete, a team, another coach or is head coach to an organisation or national federation it is essential to have input from those performance related support services that will enrich the athlete's performance plan. In my opinion it is not necessary for the coach to be an expert in all or any of these areas. What is necessary is that the coach understands what the various performance related advice can contribute to the development and performance of the athlete, team etc. and how each input can fit with the others. The coach must then deliver, on the basis of that collective input, the best plan for the person or persons being coached.

In business the same principles apply. Effective outcome in exercising synthesis skills will be the outcome of putting a tick against all of the following:-

1. Does the performance-related intelligence exist?

2. Is this intelligence available/accessible?

3. Is it accessed?

4. Is it understandable and understood?

5. Is it translatable to possible courses of action?

6. Is there competence to select the best course of action?

7. Is the course of action delivered effectively?

Synthesis skills are developed through study of the areas which may offer relevant performance-related input to the overall coaching process. On this platform, experience should be gained in using that input by working with someone who is already experienced and being guided or mentored by them. Finally, there must be constant practice in 'joining up the dots' of the growing number of potential inputs.

• Leadership
In the one-to-one coach-athlete relationship in individual sports it has always been the coach's role to lead the coaching process. It is a relatively recent concept however, that this role should also include leading those who have input to that process. Even in team sports it may not be the case that coaches are strong in all skills required of a quality leader and leading a team of players is not the same as leading a team of technical and non

A good coach will make his player
see what they can be rather than
what they are.

Ara Parasheghian[3]

A coach is someone who can give
correction without causing resentment.

John Wooden[4]

Coaches must know what they know;
they must know what they don't know;
and they must know who does!

Frank Dick

technical staff.

Formerly, some coaches in individual sports almost made an art form out of being maverick kind of characters who distanced themselves from the idea of being part of a team; whether leading the team or being a member of one. Today, however, it has become extremely important to understand the value of being strong in leadership skills and exercising these to get the best out of people individually and collectively as teams. The personnel who provide performance related services input, must be led as a team and their endeavours harmonised into the right product and or service for the athlete or team being coached. This means sensitive relationship management of people who may be very strong-willed individuals. They may themselves be highly respected leaders of teams in their own field, and being led may not sit comfortably with them. Their opinions may not normally be required to fit in with those of others. High status sometimes exaggerates egos and it demands quality leadership to help blend these within a cohesive and co-operative team.

Much of what constitute leadership skills are general, so in addition to personal strategy, learning them is often through lectures and courses involving multiple disciplines and occupations. I think this is really valuable as it introduces diverse mindsets as part of the learning mix. Experience, as always, is a great educator when reinforced with guidance and mentoring inputs. All of these, of course, become components of the leadership development journey described in Chapter 3.

• Coach's intuition

This is about subconscious intelligence and is sometimes called 'the coach's eye' or 'gut feeling'. It is now often the case that subjectivity is considered of less worth than objectivity in making decisions about people.

Decision makers are criticised for acting on what they instinctively feel is a right decision rather than waiting for scientific evidence. But Freidrich A Hayek[5] puts things into perspective:

> *'If we stopped doing everything for which we do not have the reason, or for which we cannot provide a justification ..... we would probably soon be dead'.*

Many of the judgement calls and decisions we make are due to intuitive response on reading a situation, the 'gut feeling' referred to in Chapter 4. Recognising the situation and choosing the response is certainly not always something learned from a textbook. It may best be learned through experience and often through working with someone whose own experience was their teacher. For this reason, I am convinced that it is best learned through some form of apprenticeship. By this, I mean something like in former times when young aspiring artists would learn their trade by working with established artists, as in Leonardo da Vinci learning in the studio of Andrea del Verrocchio.

In these situations the student is not only being tutored in learning the skills of their trade but watching what the teacher does and how they do it and noting the decisions made in creating excellence. They will frequently ask why the teacher did it this way, or why they did not do it another. Good observation, each note, each answer is part of a chemistry that will shape their future judgement calls and create the climate that will encourage intuitive thought to grow as a strength. This is not about copying a more experienced person, but learning from the experience of that person or persons through asking challenging questions. We should not trivialise gut feeling in the process of decision making in any field of endeavour. Developing it to be a powerfully effective competency area is something we cannot sensibly afford to neglect.

Characteristics of Great Coaches

The best coaches are easily identified in any organisation.

- They keep everything aligned between agreed values and vision.

- They are excellent communicators and, to quote Alex Ferguson, *'say just enough to get through'*.

- They give each person and the team the right size of mountain to climb so it will always be a stretching challenge.

- They prioritise developing a person's strengths. Weaknesses only become priorities if they interfere with the person delivering their strengths or if they compromise delivery of other team members' strengths.

- They plan backward from the goal and are strong in organisation.

- They have a double vision where they can focus on taking care of business today, while preparing for new arenas tomorrow. When they talk selections, they are already thinking successions.

- They contain their emotions within a channel, which those they coach rely on to bring robust stability, whatever happens. So they may celebrate but won't jump over the moon when there is success; and they empathise but don't show despair when things have not worked out. (Well, not publicly anyway!)

- They are strong-willed, resolute and unwavering under pressure.

- They support honest endeavour and challenge under-performance. They help rationalise and understand when falling short of the goal. They continue to coach and inspire the less able to raise their ability level. They do not tolerate persistent under-performance.

- They understand how to redirect, how to reward and when to reprimand and in doing so are fair, whilst demanding a very tight discipline in all things.

- They are relentless in challenging themselves to be even better next time.

- They see a mountain climbed as preparation for the next.

- They can exude pride and humility at the same time.

- They are winners.

Coaching Development in Business

In sport, coach development and recognition programs are a given. In business, an increasing number of progressive organisations are establishing 'Coaching Academies' or including coaching in their own organisation's 'University'. For the most part this has been a natural consequence of creating strong training programs. Where high performance is an imperative, those who demand it have a responsibility to ensure the demands are matched by higher quality training. Each role from work team member to senior leadership requires a high level of capacity in relevant competencies and ability to deliver.

To ensure such capacity and ability, each person must have opportunity to access the appropriate learning modules and progressions. In most instances, learning is a prescriptive process initially, but ultimately it must be self managed by each role holder. Each person must own responsibility for personal development. Every organisation must provide that opportunity, possibly as a mix of internal resource and external resource in the shape of dedicated modules. Sometimes, through carefully regulated agreements, it is possible to gain a recognised external qualification while improving role competencies for the organisation at the same time.

Quality coaching, on the one hand, contributes substantially to the learning process in channelling what is learned into effective action; and on the other also demands high level capacity in the competencies that go with this function. Skills, styles, systems and so on must be learned for delivering variously as a personal coach, team coach, head coach or coaches' coach; as a coach to beginners, to developers or to elite performers; in coaching the young or less young; coaching team members with disability; and never assuming that coaching men is always approached in the same way as coaching women. So coaches also need access to dedicated education.

Once this is in place, possibly associated with an agreed coach qualification/certification program, an organisation can experience a critical advantage to the learning process and to the performance of the organisation. If continuous learning and coaching is to grow and become part of the culture, it is necessary to create a program to develop and support it. Without such support, the introduction of coaching may be swimming against the tide of the culture. A dedicated academy should provide what is necessary for developing and

The toughest coach is experience.

Frank Dick

*The opposite of right is not wrong
- it's left!*

Jeanie Bergin[6]

*You get the best effort from others not
by lighting a fire beneath them, but by
building a fire within.*

Bob Nelson[7]

*Make sure that team members
know they are working with you,
not for you.*

John Wooden[8]

supporting a coaching culture.

Managers may not necessarily be coaches to everyone in their own team. It creates a strong motivational climate from the outset *if people can select their own coach,* who may or may not be their manager. Whatever the situation, all managers must develop their coaching competence and all managers must know who is coaching who in that team. Each manager will, of course, be coach to their team. For example, the Olympic relay team coach might not coach any of the athletes in the team individually but will be working with their personal coaches. The team coach then makes a cohesive unit of these contributions.

An essential feature of a successful coaching program in an organisation is monitoring and rewarding coaching effectiveness. A clearly understood system for this should be put in place early. I believe that establishing and developing a coaching academy within the organisation, which brings together the concept of a learning culture and coaching culture represents a profound benefit.

One final thought reference coaching. Experience in working with businesses leads me to the conclusion that when coaching and performance management is mentioned it implies that the person on the receiving end has a problem. Whether an athlete is a beginner or an elite performer; whether their performance is not what it should have been, or is outstanding; they will benefit from the right level of coaching. Or, think of it this way: You don't have to be sick or bad to get better!

Chapter 9

PLANNING TO WIN

The performance you deliver and its effectiveness in pursuit of your Olympic goal four years hence is the outcome of how you use every moment from this Olympics to the next. So each moment, in each competition and training unit; each campaign; each year; and the entire four year cycle must be carefully planned for you to make achieving your goal a probability. This is about meticulous proactive management of your environment to leave you free to concentrate on, and to deliver, the performance of a lifetime. We all have our own Olympic arenas in life!

A Planning Framework

The planning part of preparation can/should be framed within a simple model yet must be very thorough. Its purpose is to:

- Set the route map for achieving our goals.

- Create a supportive environment for our people to deliver the performances required to achieve those goals.

This I see as preparation *for* the team or business to achieve these goals and will be dealt with here. It is more the role of *manager*. Preparation of the team or business by coaching and developing our people, will be dealt with in Chapter 10. It is more the role of *coach*.

Planning Models

There are a number of models which provide a useful framework for interpreting the sense of order referred to on page 83.

STIR[1]

Select a problem

Target a solution

Implement a solution

Review outcome

And the more long winded:-

ACHIEVE[2]

Assess the current situation

Creative brainstorming of alternative to current situation

Hone goals

Initiate options

Evaluate options

Valid action program design

Encourage momentum

Before looking in more detail at the model I normally recommend and use, there is another acronym to help get the starting point of all planning right. That starting point is goal setting. It has been around since I started coaching; **SMART** (goals should be **S**pecific, **M**easurable, **A**greed, **R**ealistic and **T**ime-scaled). Time Manager International (TMI) Consultancy modified that by adding **E** exiting and **R** rewarding.

Specific   Make goals clear and define the desired result or outcome.

Measurable There must be a quantitative or qualitative measure so that there is no doubt what achievement will look like. This is easier when we are in the world of stop watches and measuring tapes, than when looking at, say, the behavioural goals associated with culture change, but it is always possible.

Agreed   Without this, commitment and involvement are doubtful. All involved must agree and accept accountability.

Realistic   This does not mean 'well within the comfort of our capabilities'! It means stretching them to the edge of possibility with the challenge to go beyond.

Timescaled Knowing exactly when things must be achieved is a vital discipline and, most importantly, focuses the mind on dealing with necessary tasks and actions *now*.

Exciting   It certainly helps the general motivational climate and gets stronger
buy-in when the goal and its value
inspire.

Rewarding   Not only the goal, but the journey to
get there, should, at the very least,
bring recognition, appreciation and the
reward of a genuine sense of fulfilment.

This acronym works equally well whether reference personal goals or those of the organisation.

The planning model I use is a popular one which I know has worked well with national teams and with business. It was originally the **GROW** model (an acronym for **G**oal, **R**eality, **O**ptions and **W**ill). It was the idea of coach Graham Alexander in 1984, then developed by John Whitmore[3] However, it seemed to me there was a critical component missing from the process, so I added L for **L**earning, giving it a more assertive resonance - **GROWL!** I think this is a great model in designing strategy and year plans.

Goal

1. What is the result we want in the given timescale?

2. What is the performance and performance consistency required to achieve that result, given current intelligence and diligent prognosis?

3. What are the components of performance and at what level must they be delivered to produce this performance?

Reality

4. What is the current position relative to the result sought?

5. What is the current performance and performance consistency?

6. At what level are the components now?

7. Who are the people involved now?

8. What are the presently available performance related resources?

This information is the outcome of the review process.

Options

9. What could be done to bridge the goal – reality gap?

- What could be done better or differently?

or

- What different things can be done?

10. Who are the people who could do that?

11. What resources could/would be required?

This is where really understanding the value of being adaptable and being creative counts in the planning process. All involved must be able to respond to the changes emerging from continuous review and to let loose their imagination and dreams. Particularly challenging here, are options to effect culture change.

Changing behaviours is considerably more difficult and takes longer than, say, changing motor patterns in technical skills. This is because we have spent our whole lives behaving the way we do, so that's not going to change in a few days or even months, just by agreeing it would be a good idea to do so! Our attitudes have persistently reinforced behaviour patterns which, in turn, have driven our thoughts and actions. The good news is, that by persistent practice over time, we can get there.

Ian McGeechan, when Northampton rugby coach, made it clear to his team that they had to change how they played their rugby. Their skills matched the giants of the time at Bath and Leicester but the whole mindset had to change if they were to challenge these rivals as English rugby leaders. He said the only way to get there was to persistently apply the necessary new behaviours not only in practice but under severe pressure in competition. Even if going back to the old way of doing things would win the game, they could not do that because they would simply be practicing and reinforcing the very behaviours they were trying to break free from.

That season they changed behaviours and unfortunately were relegated as the learning process took time and performance did not always produce results. Next season they were promoted, never losing a match. For several years, even after Ian moved on to coaching the victorious Lions then Wasps, Northampton challenged for the premiership title and became European Club Champions.

Once all options are considered, it's time for setting our course.

Will

> 12. What will the plan/strategy be?
>
> 13. What will be done in terms of tasks and actions and by whom?

This is serious detail. It must not, however, be inflexible. The journey from where we are now, to where we have

It's a bad plan that admits of no modification.

Publilius Syrus[4]

Planning is bringing the future into the present so that you can do something about it.

Alan Lakein[5]

It usually takes more than three weeks to prepare a good impromptu speech.

Mark Twain[6]

Good plans shape good decisions. That's why good planning helps to make elusive dreams come true.

Lester R. Bittel[7]

to get to, is very seldom a straight line affair. Just as an aeroplane must be constantly corrected in its flight path (to adjust to changing conditions) in flying say from London to New York, the same goes for plans. Hence the **L** in **GROWL**.

Learning

14. What controls/monitoring must be put in place to learn faster, adjust, adapt and move forward more effectively?

15. What personal learning plans are put in place to remain ahead of the game as coach or leader?

Every plan must have constant access to its own internal and external radar to be proactive when on collision course with a potential problem and rapidly responsive having encountered one. Our arenas are not like gliding across the flat water of a calm sun warmed lake. They are more like white water rafting in torrential rain with the wind howling and hazards everywhere. Plan as captain of that raft. To implement that plan by setting the route map, coaches do not plan forwards to the goal, they plan backwards from it. So, if this is the performance required to achieve a result, say four years from now, where do we have to be three months before that to make the final step? Then, three months before that, and so on until we are at our starting point. Then, for sure, the first step is properly aligned with the goal.

Once in place, the plan must be communicated to everyone in the organisation. Everything must be understood from values and vision; to behaviours and relationships; to purpose and actions. But communicating it, even regularly, and understanding it, is not what makes it work. That is down to each person buying into the plan **O**wning - choosing to be the winning difference; **D**eciding – making the right judgement calls; and **D**oing - delivering quality every moment of their contribution to the enterprise (see page 188). More than that, they must know how to deliver their own role and how to help others deliver theirs.

The Strategic Framework

In planning and preparing for an Olympic Games, I find the best approach is to break it down as follows. The first part covers the four years of general strategy encompassing the strategic framework and annual plans: the next homes in through the annual plan that leads into the games and the immediate pre-games period. Then, finally, there are the games themselves and minute by minute of the daily program.

The four year strategy

This has to reflect what I call a coach's 20:20 double vision. There must be perfect focus on preparation for realising the dream that is the goal in four years; and there must be perfect focus on dealing with today's milestones. Milestones are those moments where we influence what's happening right now. It's taking care of business today, this week, this month, this quarter, this year. In fact, the discipline of the plan that covers the year leading into the Games is actually rehearsed each year of the Olympic cycle. The critical result and performance objectives in themselves are addressed, while contributing to learning and preparation for the final year and the Games. Coaches also understand that what is needed technically or behaviourally to address milestones is seldom what is required to realise the dream. Future arenas will be substantially different than the arena we are in today. It won't simply be incrementally harder.

So two things are happening at the same time: doing what we will deliver today while preparing for what we will deliver several tomorrows from now. There is a balancing act here, of course, and it requires sensitive judgement. We must ensure we are addressing the changes that will get us to where we must be. It is a mistake to be so focussed on short-termism that we fail to be fit for the future. That said, you must do enough to take care of business today or you'll be out of business! It's difficult, but not impossible. The really great sports teams and businesses have worked it out. Let's become one of these greats!

How is that done? You must make sure that everyone in the organisation is on top of their 3 **R**'s. Each '**R**' stands for a responsibility.

R1 Responsibility for your own performance. Be the best you can be in your role.

R2 Responsibility for your own development. This is what keeps you ahead of the game.

R3 Responsibility for coaching/helping colleagues. Pass on what you learn.

Your first responsibility will make sure your own milestones are achieved. The second prepares you to be part of realising the dream. The third helps others to hit their milestones and is part of their development program to assist us in making the dream reality.

For the four year strategy, all fourteen questions in the **GROWL** model have been addressed so everything is covered from goals to competencies required to achieve them through carefully selected people in clearly defined roles. The strategy must include particular items with direction on how they may be dealt with. The following I believe to be critical components of a successful strategy in sport and, in a slightly different guise, in business.

- Machinery for how strategic and tactical policy decisions are made and by whom.

- A robust operational framework and how function and geographic area fit in management at all levels of the organisation.

- A co-ordinated review, monitoring and controls system from personal to organisational performance levels.

- An easily accessible and integrated continuous learning program to accommodate the beginner, developing and elite performer, whether they be athletes (work team) coaches, managers, leaders or support service providers. Whatever role our people deliver, each must have the opportunity and discipline to learn how to be better or to grow different skills. This is all about proactive performance management. In the more progressive sports and businesses, in-house 'Academies' are created to provide this service (see page 160).

- An effective communications network ensuring the right intelligence consistently gets to, and is accessed, by the right people. This means constantly addressing what are the most appropriate means of communication for a given situation. Some organisations' leadership achieve

this by delivering on a basic agreement to meet with, or call, colleagues and staff on dates fixed in their diaries. This ensures quality communication on a weekly, monthly or quarterly basis as a matter of routine. This supplements the regular communication media and conduits.

- A performance support services system that is effective in being both proactive and rapidly responsive. Quite simply, this system makes it possible for people to deliver the best performance they can by managing or eliminating any variable that might prevent them doing so.

- A national team/organisation preparation program to successfully meet the annual challenges whilst building continuous progression toward Olympic/ longer term performance targets.

- A dedicated team whose function it is to drive and monitor the culture change program. This must include champions from senior leadership.

- A 'New Thinking Group' (see also 'lateral thinking group' pages 72 and 73) who constantly trawl for ideas from inside and outside sport business as possible input to present and future strategies.

Annual Plans

The one year plan as a component of the four year strategy reflects all aspects. It has very specific annual results and performances as goals, and progresses the journey towards achieving those of the four year strategy. Again it should have certain inclusions which have been flagged as issues in sport and, in some instances, business.

- Dedicated programme and progress monitoring for new generation people. Whether the youth program in sport or the induction program in business and their follow-ons, these people are being prepared for, and to be, tomorrow's front line.

- Emphatic response to annual review, especially re-selection of players for the next year and eventual goal.

- Persistent reinforcement that every moment counts as a step in the journey, from training units to competition.

- Annual plan is packaged into six week blocks to provide a greater allocation of time unit to cover a range of development and performance-related objectives. That is because it is impossible to address them in tight week by week time windows at the same time as weekly competition challenges.

- 'Momentum Maintenance' programs to bridge end of six week, quarterly or annual cycles where the end of one brings a physical and emotional exhaustion which introduces inertia at the start of the next. The winning rhythm must be a momentum that is maintained. In sport there is some slack, of course, at the season end where there is a break before the next season. In business, as stated in Chapter 7, the next 'season' starts the moment the previous one ends! Like a 4 x 100m track relay, there can be no loss of baton speed through the changes of runner. There must be a system in place to accelerate through the end of one business year and the start of the new.

- Preparation for the varying cycles of high and low pressure competition periods (e.g. seasonal fluctuations in business) to use each part of the cycle to advantage.

- Pre-challenge briefings and rehearsal must become routine. Problem scenarios must be practiced. Specific preparation should be pursued for changing arenas, conditions, equipment etc. That also applies when competing with different opposition.

The **GROWL** model can still effectively apply to annual level and in the final year leading to the main competition target. However, because it is so important to be agile in learning fast and making rapid adjustments from what is learned, I like to use another acronym **OPERA**.

Objective	Set a clear performance objective and own responsibility for achieving it.
Plan	Set out how to achieve it from where you are now – including performance components KPI's or KPD's (see page 86). In sport this detail is what shapes the 'Performance Structure'.
Execute	Take effective action.
Review	Apply a tightly focussed monitoring program and learn fast from its input.
Align	Adjust, adapt and realign within the values and vision framework.

Of course, the essential focus is your own game, that is, of your team or business. It is the right plan, persistently through the year, to grow your own strengths and work to eliminate any vulnerability. It is the right tactic to play your

First build your castles in the air, work out how to put the foundations in, and bring in a construction team!

Frank Dick

You must know his game to anticipate his moves and that is how you will give him a problem he cannot solve.

Boris Becker[8]

Knowing yourself and knowing your enemy, in every battle you are victorious.

Sun Tzu[9]

Preparation turns a situation into an opportunity; and an opportunity into an advantage.

Frank Dick

own game and maximise its advantage as you impose it on the opposition.

So what is the right thinking in preparation? The legendary basketball coach, John Wooden (UCLA Bruins), who led his team to ten NCAA titles in twelve seasons, made that plan and tactic his exclusive focus. He never once scouted opposing teams. Yet he would coach his players on the court, to be alert in spotting an opponent's mistakes and weakness, and have the strength of character to capitalise on them. The speed at which the coach or the player reads the game, a particular situation or an opponent, and then responds effectively, is a critical differentiator in going for the win but maybe you can give yourself an edge.

Boris Becker, Wimbledon champion, saw it this way. When the ball is moving between you at around 150kph, you must anticipate what your opponent's next move will be. You must know him. You set him a problem and you know which best option he will use to respond in trying to make a problem for you. You must know his game to anticipate his moves and that is how you will give him a problem he cannot solve. The right thinking is, I would suggest, as advised by the Chinese warlord Sun Tzu. *'Knowing yourself and knowing your enemy, in every battle you are victorious.'*

When competing in the international arena, prepare for competing at different times in the day: for time changes; for temperature and humidity extremes; for altitude, etc. Also included here is acting on medical advice concerning local health issues e.g. allergy risks, need for immunisation shots, etc. Health and wellbeing monitoring is part of each person's personal development and performance planning. Personal maintenance is an essential given the wear and tear of addressing all the tough stuff in our arenas. An annual general health check is surely as important as getting your car serviced! Athletes have one Olympics every four years. In business, your Olympics is every week. So personal maintenance is not a 'nice to have'! It is a 'need to have.'

Homing In

Because of your meticulous planning for the four year Olympic cycle and the progressive annual plans; and because you have inbuilt learning through the experience of effectively executing those plans, all is in position for setting out your plan for each member of the team and for the team to deliver performance excellence on the day. The final planning for the team has one objective to ensure that all those variables to support the team's performance are in place; and all those which will not are eliminated or managed to advantage. Just as no two arenas, championships, or seasons are the same, nor are business campaigns, whatever the timescale. So dealing with the variables is essential. Because absolutely nothing must be left to chance the team coach and management team will work to their sport arena (and occasion-specific) checklist. That checklist has been established over several campaigns and will continue to be refined in this campaign and those to follow. The planning to date will have ensured that:-

- In the two-year run-in your athletes/players and staff should have competed at some point with the most serious opposition and at least have detailed intelligence of those good enough to be your opposition. Where there are several rounds e.g. grand slams in tennis, or stages of selection in bidding for business, this is really important. A top seed who does not have intelligence of players in the early rounds can be caught out by a little known player who sees this match as the final and will die to win it!

- Again in those two years, for athletes/players and staff, training will have become harder than the competition itself and now will have been tapered to maintain a readiness for peak performance in the face of whatever is offered by the challenge of this arena.

So the checklist will, at the very least, cover these points in preparation for the Olympic athletes' team. Because nothing should be left to chance in ensuring business teams are 100% ready for whatever they will encounter, there will also be points for them in the following:

Connecting

- Role clarity of all involved in the enterprise including where flexibility must be exercised. It is also useful to prepare in advance those who will substitute for which role in the event that this is necessary. This is normally clear for the athletes but should also be clear where staff may have to stand in for someone for some reason.

- Procedures for making and communicating any time-table or technical changes.

- Security accreditation situation to allow all athletes and staff to be where they need to be.

- Protocols and courtesies appropriate to local culture.

- Rapid communications and ease of contact system in place for all staff. Buddy system in place for athletes.

- Minute by minute duty rosters in place daily to ensure everyone is in the right place doing the right job at the right time. This covers pre, during and post competition (see also figure 16 page 186).

Competition issues

- Rules of engagement specific to this competition.

- Venue check – including, where appropriate, such things as dimensions, surfaces, equipment, fit with agreed/regulation specifications, temperature, wind directions, line of sight factors, sun angles, shelter, hazards/distractions, altitude etc. If altitude is a factor, a very specific and regulated preparation program is required and arrival at the competition venue afforded carefully calculated lead time. Where warm up facilities are available, do they afford the same conditions as the competition arena? If not, negotiate longer practice time in the arena.

- All timetabling relating to the team and to the competition.

- Pre-competition technical meeting preparation and outcome communications

- Training arrangements.

Medical related

- Anti doping testing procedure.

- Medical issues and letters of clearance must be available in the relevant language to avoid any embarrassments.

- Local medical hazards must be known and measures taken to reduce/eliminate them.

Kit and comfort

- Kit and personal equipment specific to the arena and occasion.

- Replacement kit and equipment available and accessible.

- Accommodation:- rooms, bed sizes /mattresses, climate, noise and pest control.

- Nutrition:– menus, drinks and refreshments (also at training and competition venues). Some professional sports may bring own nutritionists and/or chefs. Some bring own bottled water. If ice is used in drinks, the source of the water must be known to be clean.

Major competitions can be anywhere in the world, so travel and time change must be planned for and managed effectively.

Adapting to the change

- If a journey of two hours or less and time change of one hour maximum, travel the day before competition.

- With longer distances, for every hour of time change allow one day of adaptation time at the destination venue.

- For journeys of eight hours or more, allow an extra day. So if flying from London to compete in Vancouver nine days should be allowed between travelling and competing (eight hours time change plus one hour for travel).

- Due to tight schedules, where it is not possible to consider so much adaptation time, it is best for athletes to fly in, compete within 48 hours and then return. What you don't want is for the energy-sapping process of adapting to time change to kick in. Either compete before it does, or take the necessary adaptation time.

- Adaptation to time change is very closely related to eating patterns. As early as is reasonable, athletes are encouraged to fit into the pattern that will apply at the destination. Little food should be taken in flight – fruit, vegetables and light fibre foods are best options. Gravies, sauces and rich foods should be avoided.

Coping with travel

- People dehydrate in the very dry air conditions on flights. For every hour they should drink 0.5 litre of water or a still drink. Carbonated drinks are less effective for rehydration. Because lifestyles now mean central heating or air conditioning in our living and working conditions, we should be drinking at least 1 litre of water every day. We can quite easily become even slightly dehydrated and performance suffers. Alcohol and caffeine encourage dehydration so should be avoided, certainly during flights.

- Hydration also has a critical role in acclimatising to temperature change. Heat and/or humidity adaptation programs must be introduced well before the competition. It is an energy draining process so the immediate pre-competition period should not be seen as a heat adaptation opportunity.

- Unless using time to sleep, long flights should be punctuated by walking about the plane and stretching every 60-90 minutes. If there is a refuelling break on a long haul, use the time to walk or jog and stretch for 20-30 minutes and, if the facilities are there, shower before getting back on the flight.

- Travel wear should be comfortable and loose. Always wear elasticated/pressure socks on long haul flights.

It is now common practice when competing where there will be a time change of three or more hours, to go to a pre-competition holding camp. The same attention to detail in terms of training facilities, conditions and equipment used in preparation for the training venue also apply to the holding camp. Failure to do so not only puts the team at a disadvantage in their final preparation, but can create a fragile motivational climate. I believe that may have been at least in part behind the highly publicised events with the Irish team before the football World Cup in 2002. Choice of holding camp venue must allow optimal quality training and regeneration conditions within the same time zone as the competition venue, whilst requiring minimal travel stress in moving on to the competition venue.

On the Day

No matter how carefully you have planned and implemented the strategy over the years, months and even the final days of preparation, nothing is assumed on the day. By having runs through with everyone involved the previous day, each moment of the competition day is prepared for – from wake-up call to managing what happens after the competition is over. Everything is focussed on leaving the athlete, or team and those

Figure 16

Championships
Daily Competition Schedule

Event	Athlete & number	Time departing village	Kit & equipment check	Transport check	Coach	Physio & Doctor	Time warm up check	Time report	Time competition	Draw	Manager (post-comp)
	Basic logistics and checks to ensure athletes have all they need to compete. Sometimes wake up calls and companion at pre-event meal included.					Final preparation for the competition. This means physical, mental and emotional conditions are right for the fight					Debrief and ensure safe return to village/house

involved in supporting their endeavour with nothing more to do than perform at their best.

This is why I love studying the detail of those who plan and deliver big conferences or events. Their running order comes down to second by second action and by whom it will be taken. I am mesmerised by the moment by moment professional process detail of everything from the orchestration of an Olympic opening ceremony to that of a hospital operating theatre. Although there is no way I could ever match such benchmarks of excellence, I believe everyone in the team must receive a daily schedule to cover those athletes and support people involved on a given day. I use the format for major championships as set out in figure 16. When it comes to critical days in business, there should be a similar approach to preparing for and debriefing after.

I have looked at preparation for the team from the point of view of sport because it is my background. Of course, this is very specific in its detail. The way I see it is that I owe it to my athletes and to the badge they wear to give them the very best climate for their personal performance excellence. Likewise, everyone in business should be given the best possible climate in which to perform through meticulous preparation. It is a critical role of leadership and management. We must deliver this in practice. The daily business arena, the project challenges and the long duration campaigns must each be planned for, prepared for, delivered effectively and learned from. It is a puzzle to me if that approach is not instinctive in business even for such things as client pitches, or negotiations or the particular mountain we have to climb this week, as opposed to the same week last year, or last week.

If we are to be winners persistently that is the way it must be. If it is not instinctive today, is that because it is not the way we normally think and act in applying our business plan, this year or, indeed any year? Is it because this is not within our business behaviour mindsets, or because it is simply not part of the culture and overall strategy? All these things are related. Of course it is a really tough process to change things so this level of preparation becomes instinctively the way we do things around here. But we can do this and free every one in the team to perform at their brilliant best. To quote Henry Wadsworth Longfellow:

> 'The heights of great men reached and kept, were not obtained by sudden flight, but they, while their companions slept were toiling upwards in the night.'[10]

That's what planning and preparation is all about and it joins up the dots from culture to how we use every moment in our arena.

Chapter 10

PERFORMANCE DESIGN

It is our extraordinary capacity to adapt that allows us to take on tougher and tougher challenges. Adapting to each challenge prepares us for the next. Because such challenge can impact us mentally, emotionally or physically, preparation planning should be designed accordingly. It must also take account of the cumulative effect of all stressors and their drain on adaptation energy. The balance of cumulative stressors and recovery is critical in building performance excellence from basic skills to persistent wins.

Own, Decide, Do

Once selected, preparation of the team starts with preparation of each athlete to deliver performance excellence personally and/or in their team role. It also starts with preparation of every coach, manager, leader and support services team member who put the team in that arena. Whether working with people in the 'on the field' or 'off the field' team, the outcome of this process once again is about **O**wn, **D**ecide, **D**o. Having introduced this idea from time to time through 'Winning Matters', it might be worth elaborating farther on what it means.

Own

This is about taking responsibility and being accountable. We have a choice to see ourselves as being carried along by life's flow, like a twig in a river, or as being a shaper and influencer in our own life and that of those about us. It is my guess you are the latter. You have taken ownership of your life. That means you look for opportunity in each moment of your life's arena to turn it to advantage. You see these moments as yours to use and in doing so enrich your life's journey and that of those whose lives you touch. Whether as a parent, coach, teacher, manager leader or anyone who develops or prepares others for whatever their life's arenas are, your first objective is to give them the same sense of ownership that you enjoy. As suggested by the coaching process, they must be equipped to become the best that they can be on their own. Then you must stand out of their light.

Decide

Chapter 4 looked at the business of decision making in detail. When unleashing your people to make decisions it is sometimes tempting to judge them as good or bad decision makers according to whether or not the decisions are the ones we would make! But in preparing people to take ownership of decision making, you need to encourage difference. You need them to take considered and responsible risks in their decision making to turn each minute of opportunity into a winning difference. If everyone we coach can only make the same decisions we would make, then how can they or the business/team make progress or make a difference?

Do

Ownership and judgement calls in decision making count for little if the competencies are not there to deliver the appropriate action. That means skills and fitness to execute the action effectively and excellently must be developed in those who will do so. But, of course, having the competencies means nothing if no-one takes ownership or decision making is poor. So there's a symbiosis to all of this. These three behaviours are, I believe, fundamental for all of us.

Adaptation

I suggested in Chapter 1 that your life is like a three lane motorway and that what happens in one lane effects the others. So it is not only about training the physical, it embraces the mental and emotional. Nor is **ODD** only for and with the team, but for life. Attitudes and behaviours are all being shaped in the process. Preparation is about the whole person.

But why? Each of us is made up of three inter-connected influences shown in figure 17, the physical, the mental and the emotional. We are constantly being bombarded by different stressors mostly without us inviting them to do so! Inside, the health of the cells influences the health of the organs which influence the health of the fluids which influence the health of the cells. I'll call this the adaptation cycle.

When stressors bombard us, the adaptation cycle becomes agitated to cope with elements the cycle recognises to be a threat to the system. That is called stress; and that's as it should be. We need that to challenge the system to adapt. The adaptation process is a response to a recognised threat. It equips us to be better prepared for such threat next time. What we don't want is distress, where the system is persistently ill-prepared for the stressor bombardment because the system is then not coping and fails to adapt. The good news is that the adaptation cycle is an intelligent system

Figure 17

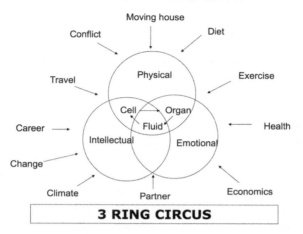

CUMULATIVE EFFECT OF STRESSORS

3 RING CIRCUS

and works very effectively given the right rhythm of stress and regeneration. Of course, I am painting a very general picture here, but you will already be aware of specific examples – such as the immune system.

So let me continue in general terms. The horizontal line O-O in figure 18 is your current status. When you apply a stressor the system fatigues. The stressor might be, for example, a strength training activity or a business challenge. When the stressor is withdrawn, the system recovers but not just to the original base line of current status. It goes above it. This is called 'over compensation'. It is as if the system realises its defences have been challenged and recruits more resources to be better prepared should the same challenge come again.

In a well thought out and constructive training program or carefully planned business programme the next and tougher stressor is applied when the peak of recovery in overcompensation is reached. That then becomes the new base line of adapted status. This process is

Figure 18

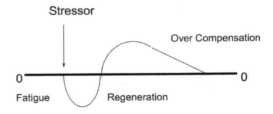

continued and progress is made up to around six weeks, when the effect of adapting to the stressor peaks (figure 19). The system no longer recognises it as a challenge to progressing adaptation. At this point, in sport, the stressor must be changed to provide a raised level of challenge. Coaches refer to this as 'system shock'. There is a dip and then progress is again made. If this process of loading the system does not permit recovery above the base line of current status, or the new adapted status, the system struggles when the next stressor is applied. So it is ill-prepared and cannot cope. To continue loading,

Figure 19

Performance

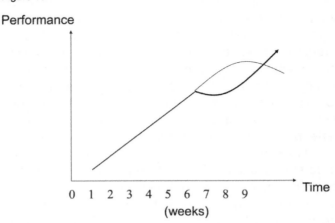

192

clearly, is not sensible. This is all very simple when taking one stressor at a time but that is not how it is in real life. The stressors included in figure 17 and any others you care to add can all be impacting on us at the same time. To make things more complicated, each may have a different timescale to recover into over compensation!

The energy required to fuel the adaptation cycle is general. There is not one tank of fuel for strength, another for burning the midnight oil, another for dealing with emotional trauma and so on. There is just one tank and it does not have infinite capacity. So, a stressor that impacts you emotionally, say, can effect you physically, because it drains your adaptation reserves. It is essential, then, that in addressing the complex of stressors which can occur across all three lanes of our life's motorway we must consider how best to prepare for development and performance in each. This 'holistic' approach to preparation, in looking at the whole person and situation, is normal in sports coaching and should be normal outside sport. Coaches prepare athletes to keep all three lanes in good shape, which, as suggested in Chapter 1, ensures you travel well. That should apply to all of us whatever we have in our three lanes.

Regeneration

But this has all been about stress and stressors so far. What about regeneration? Going back to figure 18, it is clear that without recovery into overcompensation there cannot be progressive adaptation. Ensuring proper recovery through planned regeneration is, then, very important. The problem comes when we repeatedly fail to get into overcompensation. At first the system struggles then, as already mentioned, stress becomes distress and this leads to progressive breakdown in the system. This can creep up on us without us being aware of it. We have reached a point in most of our lifestyles where there is little time for finding sanctuary; for taking regular time out to draw breath physically, mentally or emotionally to recharge our batteries. We simply occupy every moment with tasks to do for work, for others, but not for ourselves (see the 'Inside Lane' in figure 1 page 10).

We persistently take on more and more stressors either because we think we can or because we think we have to, but the cumulative stress of this eventually has serious consequences. It is like the story told of a frog in a pot of water. Frogs adapt to their surrounding temperature because they can. If the heat is gradually increased the frog adapts until it clearly has fatal consequences. I guess you think I am exaggerating. Well, we may not take things to the frog's unfortunate level, but we can certainly threaten our wellbeing! The point I hope to make here is that we must be more careful in getting the right balance between stressors and regeneration in our lives.

Does it really matter? Next time you are on a flight somewhere, ask yourself why the flight attendant during the safety instruction asks you to ensure you put on your own oxygen mask before you attend to anyone else's. It is because if you don't look after you - you cannot effectively look after others. If you don't look after you or your lane - how can you be effective in the other two lanes? So, the question is not 'does that really matter?' but 'do you really matter enough to you?'

Designing the development and performance plan for individual team members means applying the **GROWL** model to each person. Each has their own goals in terms of development and performance needs, one size certainly does not fit all in personal development. In a team, that plan is set within the context of the team's goals, and may, in turn, be set within the context of the organisation. Because a winning team must have a wide range of options to be flexible, versatile, adaptable and creative in its game plans, each team member must demonstrate such characteristics. That must be the focus of each person's plan as must the **ODD** idea in reflecting a holistic approach. In an ideal world the personal development and performance plan is not only about life in sport or business. It is also about preparing to live a better life.

So, what must be built into our lives is regeneration time. Don't wait until you are tired to take a break. If you do, you have probably been underperforming for some time. Nor should you think that by working non stop till the pre-arranged vacation you will get the shot of regeneration you need to regain your competitive edge and full fitness. You might be too exhausted to enjoy or benefit from most of it. You might even, like many people, be so low in energy that your immune system is exposed, and spend some of your Christmas break felled by a cold or flu or some other stray virus. In a well designed personal development and performance plan, a coach will ensure that 'you time' is built into your plan so that you can regenerate regularly. This keeps all three lanes operating effectively and efficiently: you perform better persistently, and for sure, you enjoy a better quality of life.

Performance Build

Coaches build performance in seven steps.

1. Learn and persistently practice quality technique(s)/skill(s)
This is about getting the basic skills and the fundamentals right from the outset. If this part of the performance build is flawed, everything that follows is about compensating

The expectations of life depend on diligence; the mechanic that would perfect his work must first sharpen his tools.

Confucius[1]

The quality of your life is in direct proportion to your commitment to excellence, regardless of your chosen field of endeavour.

Vince Lombardi[2]

To a winner, extra practice is a reward, never a punishment.

Frank Dick

The difference between try and triumph is just a little UMPH!

Marvin Phillips[3]

for that flaw and wasting time and energy trying to put it right later. Somewhere among the young people who show an aptitude for a sport are those who will be talented and on whom the future of the national team will depend. If our aim is to be winning in the world's arenas, it starts by making sure they are given the best situation and best coaching to establish the correct skills and attitudes from the moment they are in our care.

Once learned, the highest quality of skill must be maintained. To do so there must be constant realignment with skill excellence. That realignment is necessary, because in the rough and tumble of competition during a season, compensatory actions can creep in; corners are cut, and so on. If that situation is allowed to grow, whatever your role in your arena, you are compromised in your effectiveness. In a team situation, the team is compromised too.

So Jack Nicklaus would spend weeks with a professional realigning his swing in the end of year break. Katarina Witt spent at least 30 minutes rehearsing basic techniques on the ice before every practice or competition. If we want our people to be the best in their role – the same applies for them. It is for this reason that I believe beginners in sport and inductees in business must have the very best coaching in their early involvement and development. We cannot build greatness from a weak base. Induction programs in business should be delivered by experts in working with beginners or newcomers so that they can make effective contributions and add value to the team and business early and persistently.

2. Develop a fitness that generates consistent technical effectiveness

This is where technical skills become robust. In this way high quality performance is there consistently: in practice and in competition, whether in a first round or final; at the beginning of the season or the end; every moment of every day of the working week, every week of the year. In sport this is where a foundation of strength, endurance and joint mobility is established. It is where a discipline is established to do the basics well every time. Business skills must be equally robust.

As John Wooden advised, *'if you keep too busy learning the tricks of the trade, you may never learn the trade'*. It is also where the work ethic is given root. 'Doc' Councilman coach to USA's 7 gold medal swimmer Mark Spitz commented: *'With intelligent, hard work, each can achieve the best that is within him or within his team, and this is the standard he will be measured by, both by other persons and himself.'* In business, that discipline, that work ethic, are essential building blocks in developing staff, whatever their role in the organisation from beginner to senior leadership.

3. Develop a maxim speed that does not compromise technical effectiveness

Speed in performing effective technical skill is often the critical differentiator between greatness and mediocrity in the arena. Attempting to increase a speed of execution without maintaining technical quality is, however, disastrous. Introducing speed without fracturing the integrity of technical skill is achievable given carefully judged increments of stimuli to do so. So it can be trained. There is often a test of patience in this, both for coach and athlete. The exercises and practices may be right but the athlete may not be ready to benefit from them. Sometimes that patience requires going back a few steps in fitness development to make sure the athlete is ready for all stages that follow. Sometimes it is a different kind of patience. Mark Twain[4] summed that up:

> *'When I was 18 years of age, I could not believe how stupid my father was. When I was 21, I could not believe how much he'd learned in three years.'*

No year passes in business without greater demand to reach for higher targets. By definition that means everyone in the team must do more per unit of time than in the previous year. That can mean performing faster individually and as a team without losing quality in what is done, and in how it is done. This can and must be developed through relevant training to raise the operational rhythm of the organisation. Simply asking people to work faster when they are already working flat out, does not make sense. But they can learn to work faster, given the right training. Take time to provide it.

4. Develop optimal rhythm or cruising pace

This is about competing persistently at a level close to maximum personal and/or team performance. The build through the first three steps is focussed on a speed and quality of role delivery that is better than previous best performance. No one can deliver 100% of maximum all the time. So the idea is to operate as close to that as is possible, repeatedly. What you don't want is 100% one day and 50% the next! There is a special kind of physical, mental and emotional endurance that will ensure optimal rhythm or cruising speed is maintained, and it can be achieved, through specific practice. Once mastered, the idea is to deliver this in the arena and force the opposition to compete at that level. Never go down to the opposition's level. They have practiced more than you down there, so they are better at that level! Force them to play your game, at which you are, without doubt, the best.

In Toronto at the 1993 IAAF World Indoor

Championships, Tommy Mckean, one of the UK's 800m greats in that era, had qualified for the final, having led from the start in the heat and semi final. He suggested in warm-up for the final that he might change his tactics and let someone else take the pace. 'If the race is won in 1.47.00 who can win it?' I asked him. 'I guess just me, because no one else can do that'. 'If it is won in 1.48.00 who can?' 'Well, it could probably be three guys'. 'And in 1.49.00?' 'Anyone.' I could see Tommy's logic that this change of tactic would confuse them and they would not be expecting it. 'What do they expect when you lead from the gun?' 'That I'm going for the win'. So he decided to lead from the gun and he took the title with 1.47.29. Second was 1.48.02 and third 1.48.15. There is a rhythm to winning. Make it a rhythm the opposition cannot live with. Make it your rhythm.

5. Rehearse extremes and change of pace
On such a solid platform we can grow that special set of competencies, not only to deal with the various 'what if's'? and the uncertainty of changing circumstances and unexpected hazards, but to welcome them because we can cope with them better than the opposition. We enjoy the uncertainty that defines competition because we are prepared for it.

When the weather is so bad with high winds and rain that most people will stay in bed and rest, Tiger Woods will take a bucket of balls and from a poor position will aim to get every ball within 10m of the pin. Even one outside, he considers a failure. Daley Thompson would mentally rehearse crises in situations such as two failures at his opening height in pole vault in drizzling rain and a gusting wind. He'd even perspire visualising his way through the situation. He would always come up with a winning strategy. He enjoyed the idea of being able to visualise himself overcoming the worst of situations. It was part of being better prepared for the tough stuff, than the opposition. You know that no one just lets you win. You know that events can change how the competition will be won. So they must be practiced in reality, and/or virtually and/or mentally.

In sport and in business the rules can change even after the competition has started! For example, different referees and other arbiters can interpret rules differently. Circumstances that are not within your control can have serious impact on how you operate and the game plan you will use to turn the situation to advantage. At this step, having flexibility in the technical skills you and each member of the team have, permits a versatility to change on the move and lets you enjoy that advantage. This is where you develop and practice versatility. It is where you learn to live on the edge of risk in extreme situations. In fact, you can create these extremes and change pace at will and at the opposition's expense.

6. Read the game and respond faster and more effectively than the opposition

It is the capacity to make quality decisions and right judgement calls that takes the performer to a different dimension. It is where you join up the dots quicker than an opponent; where you see the problem, the solution and what will happen next in the blink of an eye, and call the shot or take the necessary action instinctively. As suggested in Chapter 4 this is as much to do with acquiring experience to read and reject the wrong cues as it is about learning from those who have already been there and how to spot the right ones. It is seldom what is learned from books or lectures. It is often learned from simulation but it is best learned from hours of experience of being in competitive situations. It is really knowing the

If you're not practicing, somebody else is, somewhere, and he'll be ready to take your job.

Brooks Robinson[5]

Success on any major scale requires you to accept responsibility..... In the final analysis, the one quality that all successful people have is the ability to take on responsibility.

Michael Korda[6]

The first forty years of life gives us the text; the next thirty supply the commentary

Arthur Shopenhauer[7]

The price of greatness is responsibility.

Winston Churchill[8]

players in your team, their strengths, their vulnerabilities and how they respond under pressure; from knowing the opposition; and from the confidence and self belief that come from mastering the five steps that brought you to this point.

Some say they are great readers of the game because they have studied well how to synthesise the inputs to making the right decision. Some say it is gut feeling. Whatever, it is important and will change the course of events in the arena to your advantage. This is the point Alex Ferguson was making in saying, *'there comes those difficult times in a game when the imagination takes over, and wins the game for you'*. It is important to understand that this does not give license to exercise what some coaching colleagues call '3-second strategies'. This is where it looks like the best solution to you but no one else in the team has a clue of what is happening! In the 2002 World Rugby Cup Final in Australia, team captain, Martin Johnson, scrum half, Matt Dawson and fly half, Johnnie Wilkinson were all reading the game as a scenario among the 'what ifs?' rehearsed in practice as part of Sir Clive Woodward's team preparation. The drop goal that won the game was the final dot of those they had collectively joined up.

In business, everyone must have opportunity to practice quality decisions and right judgement calls under pressure. The late Stafford Taylor, in leading British Telecom's 'For a Better Life' campaign, pointed out to his managers *'Our people make great decisions in their lives. They decide to join this business; to contribute to the community; to prepare for their future. So they are good decision makers. Let's build on that through this programme so that they make great decisions for the business.'* Let's coach our people in business to do just that.

7. Win and win and win again

After all, this is why we walk into our competitive arenas in the first place. In walking into your arena, the win for you and for your team is founded on **O**wn, **D**ecide, **D**o, and built on this process. Be exceptional in the foundation and in the build.

Chapter 11

FIGHTING SPIRIT

It is an odd fact of life that most of us would spare the next generations the toughest bits of life that we have had to encounter. That may, however, be doing them a disservice. Where there is too generous support and solution on offer, there is little opportunity to learn how to address challenge. In many ways, these tough bits helped shape our competitive character, our attitude in facing difficult times, our spirit to go for the win. Preparation for the really difficult moments in the arena is not just about skills and physical preparation. Everyone in the arena has these. The differentials are attitude and mental toughness. These must be learned and developed.

A Winning Attitude

Three questions must be answered before entering a competitive arena to meet its challenges. They are the same questions whether as a member of a team or as an individual.

> What do you want?
> How much does it cost?
> Are you prepared to pay the price?

They are personal questions and can only be answered by the individual concerned. The answer to the first is at the heart of ownership. The answer to the second has very little to do with economics but a great deal to do with the sacrifices that must be made to meet commitment and dedication to winning. The answer to the third is about whether or not to go for the win whatever the personal cost and sacrifice.

These are really tough questions to answer, because they reflect tough life choices and decisions. They are part of embarking on an extremely demanding campaign, because the cost does not come down to a one-off payment. As the late Vince Lombardi, NFL's Green Bay Packers legendary coach (after whom the Super Bowl trophy is named) explained:

> *'You have to pay the price to win and you have to pay the price to get to the point where success is possible. Most important, you must pay the price to stay there.'*

This takes things back to Chapter 1 and attitude. It is about making the right choice of attitude that heads an endeavour in the direction of winning. And choices matter, according to Harry Potter's coach, Professor Dumbledore!

> *'It's by your choices that people will know who you are, not by your abilities.'*

That choice of attitude keeps in focus that, whatever the challenge, it can be done. No matter how hard, winning is possible. We can do it. It's up to us. Sometimes it takes time for the penny to drop. That choice of attitude is both important and something only the individual can control.

Wayne Gretzky tells of a discussion with his father in 1983 after a practice session before the fourth game in the Stanley Cup (this is like the equivalent of football's UEFA Champions League, but for ice hockey in North America). His father asked him why he'd trained that day, to which Gretzky replied *'Because I had to, everybody had to'*. His father responded *'Well, you shouldn't have. You wasted your time and theirs. You didn't give an effort'*. The point he was making, and which Gretzky learned fast to embrace, was that the work that must go in to achieving the great competitive goals in life, is not done because someone else says we must do it but because we choose to do it. Thereafter, he always did. That choice is part of the cost.

To win persistently in the arena means that there is moment by moment focus on quality. Quality cannot be delivered if it is not practiced in training, nor if it can't be pictured or felt; nor if it can't be made to happen. As the ability to work harder and harder grows, there will be occasions where what's done in pursuit of greater quality is actually tougher than what happens in the arena.

Performers in the business arena cannot aspire to new bench marks of quality without putting in the practice to get there. Quality does not just happen. People who believe so, are people who trust in miracles to make their way through life. Miracles are great. I love them, but you can't rely on them! No matter how talented or experienced; no matter the role from ball-boy to president, quality excellence is an outcome of preparation and relentless practice. It is surely a given, then, that there is time set aside routinely for this. This really hits home when reflecting on the mindset it requires. Vince Lombardi suggested:

> *'Fatigue makes cowards of us all…the harder you work, the harder it is to surrender… If you quit now, during these workouts, you'll quit in the middle of the season during a*

*The greatest discovery of my generation
is that human beings
can alter their lives by altering
their attitude of mind.*

William James[1]

*Courage is not the absence of fear,
it is looking it in the face and channelling
it effectively to your advantage.*

Frank Dick

*Everything can be taken from a man or a
woman but one thing: the last of human
freedoms – to choose one's attitude
in any given set of circumstances, to
choose one's own way.*

Victor Frankl[2]

A hard day is the creation of soft people.

Frank Dick

game. Once you learn to quit, it becomes a habit.'

And John F Kennedy, addressing Rice University on the goal of putting a man on the moon:

'We choose to go to the moon in this decade and do the other things, not because they are easy, but because they are hard, because that goal will serve to organise and measure the best of our energies and skills, because that challenge is one we are willing to accept, one we are unwilling to postpone and one which we intend to win, and the others too.'

That mindset is about professional pride. It is where everything that is done and every behaviour that is demonstrated is seen as a critical building block in the edifice of excellence. I occasionally explain it this way. There is a great chain that connects where we start to the goal we are aiming for. Each link in the chain comprises one of us doing our job. If we deliver excellence in our own link we give strength to those we bind with to realise our collective goal. Even if one of us fails in this we will compromise our shared endeavour. So, what sort of link are you going to be? The truth is, worthwhile goals are never achieved easily and this demands a special mental toughness. Without this, all the years of daily commitment to being prepared better than the opposition physically, can count for little.

Mental Toughness

There are several characteristics that might come under the heading of mental toughness. I think the main four are as follows:

1. Cool head under pressure

This is the ability to identify and face challenges in general, and to keep a cool head in dealing with adversity in particular. This revisits the point about seeking out tough challenges to prepare for tougher ones in the future. This character of mental toughness can be trained by doing just that. Whether facing a crisis or taking a pounding, it is tempting to batten down the hatches and to see survival as achievement. Defence to avoid further damage becomes the strategy.

But you can't go forward while standing still. If not losing is the same as winning, then a draw or tie becomes a great result. The idea is to win and what has to be done to win must be understood. You know, nothing annoys me more than to hear a commentator saying 'here we are, it's half time and Scotland is losing 2-0'. As I see it, no one can be losing at half time nor can they be winning. They only win or lose at full time! They might be two goals down but that's different. The score in a game only tells you what you have to do to win. If down two goals, what must you do to win? Score three. If up two goals, what must you do? Score four because the opposition thinks all they have to do is score three! Leads are not things to be defended; nor is it OK to see damage limitation as a victory.

In the crisis of the winter of 2008/2009, many businesses went into 'siege mentality' going into serious defence mode, cutting costs everywhere, even reducing training budgets. This was understandable up to a point but this was not about having a cool head. This was a very cold head! For a start, how can people learn how to fight back if not trained to do so? The right training must surely be a constant if we are to be victorious in any enterprise.

At a world football conference on tactics and strategies,

experts were given twenty minute slots to explain their approach to the modern game. It was the legendary Liverpool manager Bill Shankly's[3] turn and he opened with:

> *'Ladies and gentlemen. There is only one objective in a game of football; you have to score a goal. Because, unless I'm very much mistaken, if you don't score a goal, you can't win the game.'*

He then sat down!

This applies in any arena. It is what the cool head is all about. Life may not be what we expect it to be in our arena, but the game still has to be won. That may mean changing how we get points on the board, but get them we must to put the result in our favour. Part of keeping a cool head is knowing what you need to be in control of to win, and remaining in control until the win is yours.

2. Persistent resilience

Captain Sullenberger's cool headed behaviour over the four minutes following US Airways flight 1549's collision with the geese (see Chapter 4) also illustrates persistent resilience pretty well! In part, this is the 'never say die' or 'don't give up' response to knock-backs. In part, it is being proactively prepared to bounce back whatever hits us.

Some years ago, I was trying to work out just how many factors had to be considered in selecting those athletes who had potential to be really great. Believe me I had a long list drawn from opinions of experienced coaches through to very clever tests from performance scientists. I discussed the list with the late Professor Miroslav Vanek, then President of the International Federation of Sports

Hard work spotlights characters of people: some turn up their sleeves, some turn up their noses, and some don't turn up at all.

Sam Ewing[4]

Careers like rockets, don't always take off on schedule. The key is to keep working the engines.

Gary Sinise[5]

A positive attitude may not solve all your problems, but it will annoy enough people to make it worth the effort.

Herm Albright[6]

Do every act of your life as if it were your last.

Marcus Aurelius[7]

Psychologists. He said, 'you know in the old days life was so simple. In the early 20th century, France produced great down-hill skiers by taking young contenders to the top of a tough run, then coaching the fastest of those who managed to risk all to make it to the bottom. And in boxing, it was normally the young fighters who kept coming back to train, even after being knocked down often in their beginning weeks, who were the ones to go on to greater things.' What was the common factor in the selection process? Resilience married to courage. They would get the skills with the help of the coaches.

Today's world of health and safety may not look kindly on such an approach to selection! Yet, this aspect of mental toughness is clearly important and can be the difference between winning and losing. In the third fight between 'Smokin' Joe Frazier and Mohamed Ali, the two boxers had caused each other so much damage, they collapsed on to their stools at the end of the 14th round. Ali looked up at his trainer, Angelo Dundee, and said he was not able to start the final round. Dundee, he suggested, should throw the towel in. The trainer slapped Ali and told him to stand up and fight. He stood up and stood tall, the seconds left the ring, the stool was removed, the bell went to start the round and Joe Frazier's corner threw the towel in! Sometimes winning simply comes down to being willing to step up to the plate more often than your opponent and certainly to stand up more often than you are knocked down. My Dad used to say to me;

> *'Failure is not about falling off your bike.
> Failure is when you don't get back on your
> bike and pedal even harder.'*

Developing such persistent resilience and getting it 'married to courage' is comfortable neither for coach nor for learner. Fear is often mentioned in the same breath as courage. Courage is not the absence of fear, it is looking it in the face and channelling it effectively to your advantage.

This development process involves real pain at times – physical, mental and emotional. It can, of course, be practiced both in simulated situations and real situations. Some people learn this through harsh apprenticeships when ordinary tasks must be repeated several times over until the person who sets the task is satisfied with the outcome quality. As a coach there are times when you will know that your athletes have done a great job, then you will look them in the eye and say 'outstanding! – but I believe you can do even better. So let's do it again – and better'. Tough love this might be – but it shapes a winner's mind set.

3. No limits attitude

The fact is limits to performance are not real, they are imagined. We let them become limits in our mind, so the will must be there to push beyond limits to live the idea that everything is possible, if we are just prepared to face the challenge. The horizon is only the limit of what we can see. It is the start of where our dreams may take us. Before Roger Bannister broke four minutes for the mile in 1954, it appeared to be an impossible barrier. In the four years that followed there were 100 performances inside four minutes. And how impossible did it seem that man could travel into space and return safely?

World records in sport are constantly being broken, often by substantial margins. At the conclusion of every Olympic Games, coaches consider performance trends to anticipate the level of performance that athletes four years hence must aspire to, if they are to go for gold. The bar is constantly being raised. Even when rules have changed, or the conditions in the arena have changed, the performance that was good enough to win this year, will not be good enough next year.

In business it's the same, whether the challenge is personal performance, team performance or the organisation as a whole. It is always seen as something we work to go 'through' not 'to'. So, this year's target, while offering a challenge in itself, is also a launching pad for next year's. The fact that this year's targets were met (or at least threatened!) makes improved targets next year a realistic aspiration.

For continuous performance breakthroughs, we have not exhausted the physical component and have hardly tapped the components of mind and emotion. When people go through some numbers barrier or reach a level of performance that no one else has achieved, they don't just do it for themselves; they do it for all of us. They show us that it can be done. We ask ourselves 'If they can do their 'impossible', why can't I do mine?' They prove that the 'impossible' is only a figment of our imagination! Training this characteristic is relatively easy, provided those who must develop it are constantly reminded about what lessons are being learned in the process.

So when athletes have improved year on year, or month on month, on a particular tough training session, they will understand they are going beyond their own previous training limits. Since that is happening in training, it is strong reassurance for breaking the annual performance target. Training sessions are designed to improve a particular component of performance. These components are to sport as key performance indicators (KPI's) are to business. So improving on KPI's is reassurance that the year's performance target is achievable. This can be a valuable enricher of the motivational climate.

I encourage performers to look out for, and to celebrate,

all breakthrough performances by other performers and across all sport. In fact, at an Olympics, I posted other sports' medals on the track and field notice board. I wanted the track and field athletes to understand that other athletes wearing the same uniform were putting our flag on the top of gold medal flagpoles. So we were part of a winning team. We could win medals too.

And what about those limits we often impose on ourselves? Those which detract us from being mentally tough? Being gentle and considerate of others feelings in life is clearly desirable, but is not what is needed when fighting in the arena. Sometimes we have to practice having a harder edge in the arena than we are naturally comfortable with outside the arena. Yet we must not take that edge outside the arena!

Daley Thompson was pretty hard to live with as he began to focus on the battle he planned to win over the two days of the decathlon. In the Olympics, IAAF World Champions, European or Commonwealth Games, this was especially the case for those he was closest to. It was as if he was saying to himself, 'if I can be hard on the people I love, I'll have no problem in being hard on the people I don't'.

Some might consider this to be an unnecessary ruthlessness, but it can be an essential one to embrace the attitude required to win. I am not suggesting here that everyone should do this, but it might help explain some behavioural changes when people are under pressure to have the hard edge honed for the arena. The time to be nice to the opposition is not during the fight, it's afterwards. The opposition is trying to take away from you the ultimate goal you have pursued every waking moment of your life, for weeks and months and years. They cannot be allowed to do that.

Sometimes we must be able to see in the opposition's

eyes the pain we are inflicting, yet wittingly inflict more until they are finally beaten. We cannot hold back at this point or the opposition will fight back to catch us off guard. You must put them out of action. This is about assertiveness not aggressiveness. You must have the heart to finish the job.

For most of us, this is certainly not how we would wish to be seen in our day to day interaction with people. In the arena, 'to be the very best that we must be to win' may mean that this face of mental toughness is the difference between gold and nothing. Practicing to push through limits involves getting out of our depth. This is necessary in order to test ourselves in any aspect which might weaken our resolve.

4. Self discipline

This is about keeping your eye on the ball. It is about sticking to the task at hand and blocking out all distraction. Yet it is also having a restless vigilance through relentlessly exercising your personal radar, every moment of the game, to pick up on opportunity for advantage and for threats to successful pursuit of purpose.

It is a special characteristic in building mental toughness that gets people through the most brutal training sessions and has them fight to make every moment in the game theirs. That means whether it is the first or last second, the first or last metre, of the encounter. It means being in control from the 'B' in the 'Bang' of the gun as Linford Christie would insist; through to those moments described by Rudyard Kipling:

> 'If you can force your heart and nerve and sinew to serve your turn long after they are gone, and so hold on when there is nothing in you, except the will which says to them: Hold on!'.[8]

Warming up and being ready for the fight takes place before going on to the field. No one hands out time to settle. Careful preparation for the team provides a framework, but there is a personal discipline to it. A winning rhythm must be picked up early in the arena – then sustained throughout the battle. And being ready for the fight is where blocking out distraction begins. When the best former East European athletes arrived in the warm-up area, they would each isolate themselves in a quiet part of it. For 5 to 10 minutes they would off-load all life outside their immediate purpose. The bits outside were distractions that could clutter their minds. They had to be thrown out. Their immediate purpose was to win. That demanded 100% focus on a winning performance. Mostly, they won.

Distractions are anything that takes your eye off the ball. So that can be simply a momentary loss of concentration through to bringing untimely unfamiliar variables into what should be unobstructed focus on performance. This is why leaders, managers and coaches must be very clear on what is, or is not, acceptable in such situations as the balance between focus on performance and marketing, publicity or promotion. For example, it cannot possibly be sensible for players, managers or anyone who is part of a major championship challenge, to be distracted by press or media stories of future contracts or of matters that blur their focus on the goal. Concentration cannot be fully on the job at hand. It is not only those in the headlines who get hurt here. It is the entire team. It is also why blocking out distractions should be practiced, or dealt with in anticipation.

So, in business it is useful from time to time to have each member of the team go through 'what if?' situations (see page 200). Such can be simulated crisis situations; an out of the ordinary event; a change in regulations; coping with a staffing problem; dealing with opposition tactics and so on.

Some organisations put such scenarios out on pod-casts or apps as part of 'training on the move'.

In the arenas of sport, the opposition team and fans may choose to try and 'wind up' players to the point where they 'lose it' and react badly. We know this happens, so each player must be coached to handle such situations in practice. Although such treatment feels personal, it really is not - it's just that player's turn! The opposition is simply trying to make their distraction bigger than the player's focus. That can't be allowed to happen.

One other point here, is the situation of moving up into unfamiliar territory because performance excellence takes someone from one league, as it were, to another. Whether walking into an Olympic arena to compete for the first time, or being promoted to senior status in the organisation, the new environment cannot be allowed to detract from delivering the performance excellence which made that move happen.

The incredible sense of a 90,000 crowd presence, when coming out of the tunnel into the light and heat of the arena, can make knees wobble if the previous maximum crowd experience was less than 3,000! So track and field coaches sometimes arrange for their athletes to have the opportunity to run round a Premiership Football stadium in front of a capacity crowd to fully appreciate what it will feel like. Random interruptions of noise and line of sight movement can also be introduced to build focus discipline.

Simply trying to be great in a new role without rehearsing how to deal with those who are perverse can damage your overall personal effectiveness in a team. When Ronnie Irani became Essex cricket captain, he brought to this role his very characteristic passion to make things happen. That passion he visited on every player's performance and to addressing every problem on and off the field. In fact, it had him almost playing all eleven team roles and

Up is never where you are now.

Belasco & Stayer[9]

If you wait for success to happen, it won't: it's something that you make happen, or it can't be called yours.

Frank Dick

There are no traffic jams in going the extra mile.

Roger Staubach[10]

No one ever finds life worth living, he has to make it worth living.

Anon

People who feel good about themselves perform better.

Ken Blanchard[11]

taking responsibility for solving every problem himself! Unfortunately two particular players created tension in their relationship with Ronnie resulting in a deterioration of his own game during the first part of the season. The situation was resolved by picking up on advice to separate out components of the complex role of leading the team so that he could deal effectively with one issue at a time while parking the others. He practiced 'what ifs' in virtual scenarios. He then resumed his top contribution with both bat and ball and established himself as an outstanding leader.

We know in advance that people must cope with these distractions as they move into new roles, or are promoted or enter a new and tougher level of challenge. So, we must prepare people in advance so that they build the kind of mental toughness this demands. If not, they under perform, become de-motivated and in some instances walk away. When that happens, I believe the failure is ours, not the person who struggles.

Time

There are many important reasons for getting self discipline right, but I would like to focus on one in particular. It is to do with time. Excellent time management must be a given in every field of endeavour if we are to achieve our goals, or we end up chasing out tails. We know what must be done and how we must do it. We allocate time each day, each week, each month to ensure that every action is addressed, from high priority to routine low priority. Until every task is completed and every goal accomplished, we make appointments with our dreams and we keep those appointments.

But there is another time related dimension to this characteristic of mental toughness, and that is timing. As we progress to higher echelons of competitive challenge the time available to effectively address each challenge shrinks. There has to be a sharper vigilance to exercise agility in reading the game; in judging when and how to act; and in delivering performance excellence under time pressure.

It is as if at club level you have 1.0 sec; at national level you have 0.5 sec; and at international level 0.1 sec! The skills are the same, the time to deliver is not. With each level of progression, it is this narrowing of the time window that underlines Dan Topolski's[12] statement:

> 'The biggest problem always is to transfer good technique when they are not under pressure, into good technique under intense competitive pressure'.

We learn to execute the basic skills of our role, the fundamentals, perfectly through the performance build process. When the outcome is outstanding, it is because we deliver the basics with 'good technique'. If it is less than outstanding, it is seldom because of some complex mistake but a simple mistake involving the basics. Practicing these under pressure is a life long task and a major contributor to mental toughness.

Managing Motivation

Building mental toughness on top of the cumulative effect of meticulously planned training and commitment to continuous learning brings a winning attitude and a strong personal motivational climate. Those with it, radiate it. It is an aura of self belief but never arrogance. They are very aware of their achievement yet there is a humility. But this climate can be fragile, and for even the best in their field, there is a need to be reassured. In quiet moments they wonder if they can constantly re-define personal excellence and perfection. In some ways this drives them to push themselves even harder. If they feel no need to be pressured by continuing to raise their game, they must take Percy Cerutty's[13] advice:

> *'When you have made it, when you are sitting on top of the world….. you need prodding to ensure you don't fall off your perch.*
> *If no one prods you, prod yourself!'*

It is now a well established measure in sport to prepare edited DVDs of an athlete or team performing at their very best. They play it to themselves to remind them just how great they can be. What they are doing is helping keep motivation's scales tipped in their favour. I think of these scales like this (figure 20); the 'Will to Win' side should always hold advantage over the 'Fear of Failure'.

There are three parts to **'The Will to Win'.**

1. Want to win – be hungry for it.

2. Believe you can win – that needs constant reinforcement.

3. Persist until you win – bring excellence and fight to every moment until the win is achieved.

The **'Fear of Failure'** has four parts – each can be fatal to the endeavour if not dealt with.

1. Fear of losing – this is dealt with by living the definition of winning; *'be better today than yesterday – every day'*.

Figure 20

Fear of
Failure

Will To
Win

2. Fear of making a mistake – take the risk of winning here. We all make mistakes when fighting to go beyond those familiar things that were part of being good enough to compete successfully in yesterday's arenas. No mistakes, no risks; no risks, no progress. Just remember the three rules about mistakes listed in Chapter 3.

- Own up to them
- Learn from them
- Don't repeat them

3. Fear of rejection – life is full of moments where you either make the cut and get selected, or you don't. For sure, it is necessary to prepare well to make it, but if not, the worst thing that can happen is you are better equipped to face the next challenge. So go for it!

4. Fear of embarrassment – in doing things differently or in doing different things, others may not go with your new actions or ways and give you a hard time. Remember in life you are accountable only to the person who looks back at you from the mirror each morning. You know whether that person is doing the right thing or not. If the

224

face smiles – forget what others might say right now. In time they will learn! If the smile is not there, then be your own tough task master.

Keeping scales tipped towards **'The Will to Win'** sets the right motivational climate. But let me go back to the idea of self belief. I think there can be two cycles of self belief. There is high self belief (figure 21) where better performance is rewarded by recognition and appreciation and continues to grow. There is low belief (figure 22) where underperformance brings discouraging feedback and goes in a downward spiral.

The fact is that it takes very little to lift people out of the low cycle and into the high. Ken Blanchard's great line is all that we need to remember: *'People who feel good about themselves perform better.'* We each know what makes us feel good about ourselves in terms of the right words at the right time. And the right time is any time in either cycle. So just say the right words.

I believe that what can lift us in our teams and businesses is far less about motivating people than about avoiding de-motivating them. When people come into our organisation they are all highly motivated because this is where they want to be. So, if they are not motivated a couple of years down the line, it is probably not them that we should be looking at, but ourselves.

De-motivation probably begins when people feel that what they are doing is more about working to earn a wage rather than working to be the person they aspire to be. Very often this simply comes down to the person feeling that their role does not provide the challenge they need to be better. When everyone in an organisation knows that every day brings a new challenge and meeting that challenge gets them further up their own mountain; when getting there is recognised, appreciated and rewarded, de-motivation disappears. Getting to that point has to be

Figure 21

Cycle of Self Belief

Even Higher Self Belief

High Self Belief

Celebrating & Enhancing
Motivational Climate

Taking Risk of Winning.
Play Through Limits

Performance Beyond Maximum.
Great Results

Figure 22

Cycle of Self Belief

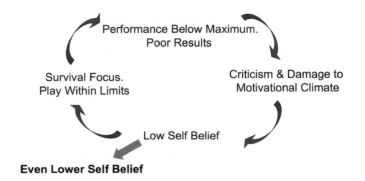

Performance Below Maximum.
Poor Results

Survival Focus.
Play Within Limits

Criticism & Damage to
Motivational Climate

Low Self Belief

Even Lower Self Belief

addressed by the organisation, which means everyone in it! And that is part of being prepared to pay the price of going for the win.

Mental toughness is something we each must develop to make our own and our team's performance all that they must be to win persistently. It grows, given the right motivational climate and each of us can make it right. So, when your footstep echoes in the tunnel and you feel the crowd's anticipation of your arrival in the arena, you smile on asking yourself the same two questions that so many Olympians have asked themselves at that moment. You know the size of challenge. You know what has to be done and that only one person will stand on the podium. So – *If not you, who? If not now, when?*

Chapter 12

ADVANTAGE YOU

We can choose or change our attitude. We each manage our own motivational climate. And this all starts with knowing who we are and what we have to do at being better at being ourselves. We can win every day. Once that is in place, we may raise our game even higher, when we see ourselves as part of belonging to something bigger than ourselves. There is immense value and advantage in this. It is the badge we wear and can be the brand name of the business we work for, the club or nation or culture whose colours we wear. It is a concept we give life to and that gives us life.

Motivation Climate Control

When things do not work out the way we intended them to today, we can feel pretty flat. It is as if what should have been a great day has been hijacked by the bits that did not go right. My two daughters, Erin and Cara have a system for dealing with this. Whoever feels flattened takes a piece of paper and makes two columns. On the right she lists everything that went right that day; on the left she lists those things that did not. On every occasion there are far more things in the right column compared with the left! It then becomes clear that the day was, in fact, pretty good and full of substantial achievement, not one of failure.

I believe that this is true for everyone. Each day is achievement rich because you make it that way. Glitches there may be and deal with them we must; but spoil the sense of achievement they must not. The right column for you will be full of right decisions made on things you owned and of tasks successfully completed. Some will be major; some will be milestones; some will be 'one offs', some will be done regularly. All will be done excellently. All should be recognised and appreciated. In fact, we need that. Those cultures which enjoy a motivational climate where this is understood reflect those behaviours that celebrate achievement, support endeavour and challenge under-performance.

Celebrate achievement
Where this has become instinctive in a culture, achievement is celebrated wherever it is recognised. Nothing is taken for granted. No improvement or advantage passes without an appreciative comment. Because everyone aspires to personal excellence and to winning, each occasion when it happens in the team or organisation is an opportunity to spread assurance. The spirit of celebration is in sincere open appreciation.

Support endeavour
The energy sapping fight to achieve a goal and to keep on achieving them, carries a heavy cost. People will stumble or even get hurt in their fight. Moreover, the process can take some considerable time. It is important for them to feel that colleagues and, especially, those who manage and lead, understand this and cultivate a very real sense of being on the same side in supporting them.

Challenge under-performance
No one tries to get things wrong; nor do they try to under

perform. They are trying to do the right thing and if it is not working out for them and we see this, they will expect us to challenge them so that such problems are not repeated. Underperformance cannot be allowed to keep repeating itself because it hurts the person involved and compromises the collective endeavour.

Being Valued

All of this is about ensuring that people are valued for what they do. People need to feel valued. You and I have that need. We enjoy it when we receive a word or a note of congratulation; a pat on the back; a smile and nod of appreciation or thanks. We are grateful for encouragement to keep going through disappointments, frustrations and tough times. We feel a sense of mutual respect when reminded that we can do better and when we are challenged and coached to do so. Because we feel good about ourselves when valued, we know that also applies to those around us, so we make a point of valuing them.

When we step back to pursue moments of personal reflection, our need to feel valued can go beyond being valued for what we do, to being valued for who we are. You are more than a title or a name and someone who has done a great job. You are you! But what does 'you' mean? Who are you? Is it important to know the answer to that question? I think so, if, for no other reason than to ensure you remain a winner. I mean, how can you continue to be better today than you were yesterday; to continue being better at being you; if you don't know who 'you' are in the first place? Sallie Krawcheck[1] certainly believes it is important:

> 'Truly knowing myself for the first time changed
> my life and gave me confidence to accomplish
> more than I ever could have imagined.'

I have listened to many experts present on this subject, yet found myself switched off because I did not feel that they got me any closer to a sense of personal discovery! It needs someone you trust to help you step back and take the personal 'time out' or 'pit stop' to explain things and to challenge you to challenge yourself, to know you.

Caroline McHugh, internationally renowned speaker and founder of ID-ology, the training and personal development company, understands this more than anyone I've met. Caroline coached me in this and I certainly needed coaching! I guess the problem for most of us is getting to grips with the fact that there are different perspectives on who we are. She suggests four when addressing the subject of the art of being yourself at work:

Perception is what people think of you.

Persona is what you would like other people to think of you.

Ego is what you think of you.

Self is what makes you, 'you'.

• Perception

As the saying goes, 'perception is reality'. It is this that shapes the opinion others have of you. Perception, of course, is more than what people see and hear. It is how they spin things on the basis of their previous experiences, personal preferences and so on. So, different people may have a different perception of who you are. To reduce the influence of such subjectivity when, say interviewing people for a job, numerous test batteries have been designed to create a more accurate perception of who you are in terms of suitability for the role in question.

• Persona

In the Beatles song 'Penny Lane', the nurse thinks that

Why not be oneself? That is the whole secret of successful appearance. If one is a greyhound why try to look like a Pekingese?

Dame Edith Sitwell[2]

When you believe in who you are, you will believe in what you do and how you do it.

Frank Dick

People know you for what you've done, not what you plan to do.

Anon

If you don't like something change it; if you can't change it, change the way you think about it.

Mary Engelbreit[3]

'she is in a play, she is anyway' which may have echoes of Shakespeare's observation:

> *'All the world's a stage,*
> *And all the men and women merely players:*
> *They have their exits and their entrances;*
> *And one man in his time plays many parts.'[4]*

We each have a picture of how we would like to be perceived by others. It is as if we are acting out each of our several roles in a great production. Sometimes such might be captured by the role itself; for example, a parent or partner or friend, or a position such as a doctor or HR director or teacher; and so on. We slip into and out of these roles turning ourselves at will into whatever fits the situation or the relationship we have with the persons forming perceptions of us.

Naturally and normally we will do so on the basis of strong personal values such as honesty, sincerity and integrity; and within the boundaries of social convention. So it covers everything from courtesies to demonstrating role excellence. Unfortunately, there can be clear differences in the perceptions people have of us and the perceptions we wish them to have. This can be startlingly illustrated when we compare words that we would use to describe how we think others see us with words that they would actually use to describe us. It seems to me to be pretty important that we try to close the gap between perception and persona. If not, we run the dangerous risk of creating confusions that can cause issues of miscommunication, misunderstanding of motivation and fraying of relationships.

• Ego
Unfortunately, the term 'ego' appears to get bad press! It has become a negative comment when someone is

considered to have an 'ego'. So that expression often reflects the perception of arrogance. The fact is, we all have egos. Your ego is the opinion you hold of yourself. There is, for most people, a real frankness in how we see our strengths and vulnerabilities in this opinion. It is here that personal motivation dances between intellect and emotion to ensure the radiance of self belief is not dimmed by the shadows of self doubt. Rather, it is tempered by constructed, measured modesty. Your ego is your unique, special difference.

• Self

Discovering what self means to you is something that many people do not want to make time for. Some will actively avoid doing so. Such discovery is not the outcome of some kind of scientific research or analysis. It is the outcome of deep personal reflection in our own personal space. It requires a special personal discipline of mental, emotional and physical focus; of dedicated time; of sanctuary. It seems to me that there are less and less opportunities to enjoy such a sense of sanctuary. How often do we make our personal space a no-go area for mobile phones, Blackberries etc? When do we close the open door? Where can we go to hear nothing but our own thoughts?

Making and taking time for personal reflection, contemplation, meditation or prayer seems to have decreasing priority in our busy lives, yet I honestly believe that, however we use that time, it is important that we do so. Not only can it grow a stronger sense of self value and self belief, it clearly contributes to personal wellbeing in stress management and to personal effectiveness in seeding creativity and mental sharpness. How you build this into your life is your choice and you must be comfortable with it. For me it is walking or jogging for an hour before breakfast. For some colleagues it can be sitting on a beach calmed by the rhythmic ebb and flow of the waves, or feeling the solitude and silence once they have climbed to the top of a hill, or listening to chill-out music. For others it will be discipline that meditation takes in a location that brings the peacefulness to which they wish to retreat.

Your Difference Matters

You represent a great and unique gift of energy and time. Only you have your energy. You cannot give it to someone else nor can they give you their's. And only you have your time to use it. As Martha Graham[5] explains:

> 'There is a vitality, a life force, an energy, a quickening that is translated through you into action, and because there is only one of you in all of time, this expression is unique. And if you block it, it will never exist through any other medium and it will be lost. The world will not have it'.

The gifts are for you to use to enrich the world by being the difference that only you can be. Yet some people see themselves as pretty insignificant in the great scheme of things. No one is insignificant. Everyone is precious; each can make their unique difference. And that matters.

After a thunderstorm on the west coast of Florida, thousands of starfish have been washed ashore and are stranded the length of a beach. The sun is up, the tide is out and they will die there. An old lady sees the situation and begins throwing them one at a time back into the sea to help them stay alive. A young boy spots her and asks why she is doing this. She explains why.

235

> *'That's crazy', he says, 'just look at the number of starfish on the beach. What difference do you think you can make?'*

She thinks for a moment, then picks up another starfish,

> *'Do you see the starfish I have here? I will make a difference to this one.'*

and throws it into the sea. Each of us can make a difference. It is our choice to be that difference.

Choosing to be so and doing something about it, matters. That choice is about being the best that you can be. It does not belong to someone else's time. It belongs to your's. Steve Jobs[6] explains it eloquently:

> *'Your time is limited, so don't waste it living someone else's life. Don't let the noise of other opinions drown your own inner voice. And, most importantly, have the courage to follow your intuition. It somehow already knows what you truly want to become.'*

Of course, it takes time to reach the position where we have the self confidence this demands.

The Learning Journey

I believe we can get there only as quickly as it takes to complete a long learning journey. Bart McGettrick Emeritus Professor of Education at Glasgow University explains that the journey has five stages. It is my guess that you will easily identify which stages are now well behind you. The brackets are my interpretations.

1. Learn to repeat.
   (Repeat what the teacher/book says!)

2. Learn to learn.

   (Manage your own continuous learning.)

3. Learn to do.

   (Be executive in translating what's learned into effective action.)

4. Learn to be.
   (Learn about being you.)

5. Learn to become.
   (Become the difference you can be in influencing real change.)

Being the difference may not always be recognised and appreciated, even by those who benefit directly. This is often the case where the difference is not something clear cut like making a sale or putting points on the board. Sometimes, doing something extra to support someone else make a difference, may pass unnoticed. But you will know it. You will know that it was down to you; that you made the right decision; that you did the right thing and so enjoy the really great feeling that comes with that knowledge. With or without acknowledgement from others, there is no arrogance or conceit in smiling to yourself in recognising that you made the difference today.

There are certainly no rules that prevent you being your own motivator! There exists both a pride, and a certain humility, when you know that, although it was done by you, it was not only for you. Of course achievement brings you a personal sense of reward. But there is more to making a difference than that. You do this also for what you are part of; for what you belong to.

You must do the things you think you cannot do.

Eleanor Roosevelt[7]

Quality is remembered long after the price is forgotten.

Gucci Family motto

It's not the employer who pays the wages; he only handles the money. It is the product that pays the wages.

Henry Ford[8]

Perfection is the dream; the fight to get there is the reality.

Ferrari mechanic's motto

Ask not what your country can do for you, ask what you can do for your country.

John F Kennedy[9]

The Badge We Wear We Own

By 'part of' or to 'belong to', I mean something that goes beyond the bond we enjoy with those in our team. It is what our flag on the flag pole or the badge on our shirt or the organisation crest or logo or brand stands for. I think of this simply as 'the badge'. To 'belong to' what our organisation's badge stands for means much more than wearing the same label as our colleagues.

In the movie 'The Devil Wears Prada' a young girl, Andie, has recently taken a job at a magazine. To her it is just that, a job; a source of income. Her friend Nigel suggests 'this place, where so many people would die to work, you only deign to work'. His perception of working for the magazine is that he belongs to what it stands for. The reason he is there is to give all that he is to what he believes gives so much to him and to the world. He has a passionate relationship and engagement with the badge he wears – the magazine.

When we get to such a point in establishing the relationship between a team member and the badge, whatever the enterprise, it makes a profound difference to the quality of team member input. Of course, for any relationship to be persistently effective in enriching the lives of those who share it, and in continuing the value of its purpose, it has to be worked at constantly. Relationships cannot possibly be what they must if those in the relationship take each other for granted. The idea is to put your best into it so that everyone gets the best out of it. As previously discussed (see page 129) every relationship must be worked at.

Whatever the badge, be it family, school, club, organisation, country or whatever, there must be an essential interdependence exercised by all those who wear it. The continued reinforcement of what it stands for depends on this. Your unique value in being who you are can make a difference to the badge. The value of the badge can make a difference to you. It is the commitment of each to making their difference happen for the other that ensures the badge continues to win in its arena, and you continue to win in yours. These differences do not only have impact today. They influence your life as a whole and they influence those who will follow you in wearing the badge.

There is absolutely no doubt in my mind, that in fighting for a greater purpose we fuel a higher motivation. In knowing that what we do is not just for ourselves, but for a greater purpose, a higher cause, we are given substantial advantage in our journey to be all that we are capable of becoming. We feel that the badge belongs to us; that we are the strength of its heartbeat. We ensure that the badge will enjoy even greater value beyond the contact we have with it. And I am equally certain that when we accept that the badge, through its leadership and management, is truly working for us to be successful in our journey, we lift the quality of our contribution to our endeavour for the badge. More that that, we actively enrich the culture the badge represents. The badge feels that we belong to it. In such a climate, the badge enhances the quality of our life, not only in terms of the contact it has with us, but outside that contact.

Phil Brown illustrates that special symbiosis of badge and individual. His discipline in track and field events was 400m. He certainly was a fine individual 400m athlete, running at Olympic and Commonwealth Games, World and European Championships but he seldom went far in the individual competition. In the relay however, he was a class apart. When he ran for the team, for the badge on his vest, he regularly outran those whose individual performance was better than his. It is essential that everyone who wears the badge understands this symbiosis and works to make it happen whether they are the new recruits or the well established. It is for each of us as we make our way in building our relationship with the badge to be aware of what it stands for. Each of us must understand what has gone into growing it to this point and who has made it possible. We must appreciate who were and are the heroes and the role models from beginner to leader.

In making a 100% commitment to personal development that will deliver greater and greater performance to be the winning difference, we must also ensure there is a clear perception of that commitment and of pride in belonging to the badge.

It is for those more experienced in wearing it, whether colleagues, managers or leaders, to be aware of who we are and why we choose to wear it. They promote its value to us. They do so by recognising and appreciating all those moments when we apply best endeavours to add value to it through our input. They do so by coaching us and supporting us to perform better. They do so by explaining to us from time to time what the badge stands for. Their contribution to its greatness is, for the most part, in how well each of us responds to their management and leadership.

Our contribution, whatever our role or stage of development, is to persistently raise the bar in producing personal performance excellence: For you and I to be the you and I we aspire to being. Together, we prepare the badge to be even stronger in even tougher arenas. Appreciating that each of us enjoys an interdependence with each other and with the badge that connects us, is both a reassurance and a motivation. In the awareness that we have very effectively joined up the dots in this part of our life there is motivation to look for other dots and make other connections in an even greater perspective. John F Kennedy famously said: *'Ask not what your country can do for you, ask what you can do for your country.'*

I believe we continuously ask questions of ourselves that are similar to these. We look beyond our own horizons to where being 'us' can make another kind of difference. We become winners in another kind of arena. You do so when you send off your cheque to this or that charity whether it helps someone in the neighbourhood or on the other side of the world. You don't know the beneficiary and they will never know who cared about them. But you do it anyway. You do so when you treat someone the way you'd like to be treated, not the way you have been treated. You do so when you go out of your way to make sure someone has a better day. You do so when you actively reduce your carbon footprint. You do so in countless ways. That is what I mean by 'making another kind of difference'. And you do so when you live the words of Albert Schweizer:[10]

> *'It is not always to the sower of seeds to reap the harvest.'*

I believe the harvest we reap today in the shape of the world we have; the freedoms we enjoy; the opportunities that exist to join up more dots; and the challenge to be even better at being who we are, are the fruits of seeds sown by people whose hard work and sacrifices made that harvest possible. They paid it forward and, for the most part we'll never know who they were, to thank them. Like those who made all of this possible in their time we strive to make that other kind of difference in our time - to make things even better for those who follow. We can pay it forward. But you know this. It is what winners do. This is why Winning Matters.

Without dreams, possibility
knows no excitement.
I cannot dream your dreams for you,
nor can I realise them for you.
Only you can do those things.
It is for you to excite possibility.

Frank Dick

IT'S TIME

I always feel awkward when it comes to the moments before an athlete leaves the warm up area to go into the arena. It's what to say! I've done my job as coach; the book is written. I hope it worked for you.

It's for you now to do yours – go out there, give the performance of a lifetime you've been preparing for; and win. And when you've done that, be prepared to win again, and again in all the arenas that are waiting for you, however you define them.

So do just that, be the greatest you that you can be. That's tougher than you think – because you've had to be great to win in the arenas that are behind you! But you are a winner and know what winning is – 'be better today than yesterday, everyday'. And when you do that, you'll make a difference in this world. I know you'll be a winning difference.

> So: Be breath taking in your performance in all your arenas.
> Be breath giving in the difference you will make.

WHO'S WHO

1. WINNERS WIN

1 **Don Shula** (b.1930) Former American professional football player & coach best known for coaching Miami Dolphins to two Super Bowl victories.

2 **Daley Thompson** (b.1958) One of the most successful decathlon athletes ever. Won every event entered between 1978-1988. Gold medals in 1980 & 1984 Olympics.

3 **Pierre Corneille** (1606-1684) French dramatist. (Quote from Le Cid, 1636).

4 **David Lloyd George** (1863-1945) Liberal Chancellor of the Exchequer 1908-1915. Prime Minister 1916-1922.

5 **Zig Ziglar** (b.1926) American author & motivational speaker.

6 **Oliver Wendell Holmes** (1809-1894) American author & physician.

7 **Wayne Bennett** (b.1950) Australian professional rugby football league coach & former player. Don't Die With the Music in You, ABC Books Australia 2007.

2. CHANGE TO WIN

1 **George Bernard Shaw** (1856-1950) Irish playwright.

2 **Frances Hesselbein,** The Key to Cultural Transformation, Leader to Leader, Spring 1999.

3 **Peter Michael Senge** (b.1947) American scientist & director of the Center for Organizational Learning at the MIT Sloan School of Management.

4 **Jim Rohn** (b.1930) American entrepreneur, author & motivational speaker.

5 **Robert P Vanderpoel** (20th C) American former Chicago Sun-Times Financial Editor.

6   **John Henry, Cardinal Newman** (1801-1890) Roman Catholic priest & Cardinal, a convert from Anglicanism.

7   **Mark Sanborn** (20th C) American bestselling author & noted authority on leadership, team building, customer service & change. Author of The Fred Factor.

3. LEADING EDGE

1   **Dr. Henry Alfred Kissinger** (b.1923) German born American political scientist & diplomat. Served as National Security Advisor and later concurrently as Secretary of State under Richard Nixon. Awarded 1973 Nobel Peace Prize.

2   **Peter M Senge**, The Fifth Discipline – The Art and Practice of the Learning Organisation, Doubleday, NY 1990.

3   **John Viney** (1947-2009) One of UK's foremost headhunters & author of leadership books.

4   **Field Marshal Bernard Law Montgomery** (1887-1976). One of the most inspirational British military commanders of World War II.

5   **John Buchan** (1875-1940) British polymath, novelist & politician. Served as Governor General of Canada (1935-1940). Author of The Thirty Nine Steps.

6   **Ralph Waldo Emerson** (1803-1882) American transcendentalist poet, philosopher, lecturer and essayist.

7   **General Colin Powell** (b.1937) Former American General and Secretary of State under President George HW Bush.

8   **Stephen R Covey** (b.1932) American author. Wrote the bestselling book, The Seven Habits of Highly Effective People.

9   **Michael McKinney** (20th C) Publisher & President of M2 Communications.

10 **Kevin Spacey** (b.1959) American actor, director, screenwriter & producer.

11 **Lao-Tzu** Legendary 6th century BCE philosopher of ancient China & central figure in Taoism.

12 **Harold Geneen** (1910-1997) American businessman & former president of the International Telephone and Telegraph Corporation (IT&T).

13 **Oliver Wendell Holmes** (1809-1894) American author & physician.

4. DECISIONS, DECISIONS

1 **General George S. Patton** (1885-1945) American general in both WWI & WW2.
2 **Francois-Marie Arouet Voltaire** (1694-1778) French philosopher & writer.
3 **Albert Camus** (1913-1960) Algerian-French author philosopher & journalist. Awarded the Nobel Prize for Literature in 1957.
4 **Gerhard Berger** (b.1959) Austrian former Formula One racing driver who competed for 14 seasons.
5 **Roger Steare** Ethicability, Roger Steare Consulting Limited 2006.
6 **Gilbert Keith Chesterton** (1874–1936) English author, poet & journalist.
7 **Vernon Sanders Law** (b.1930) Former American Major League Baseball pitcher for the Pittsburgh Pirates.
8 **Oscar Wilde** (1854–1900) Irish playwright, poet & author.
9 **Richard Bach** (b.1936) American author of Jonathan Livingston Seagull.
10 **Peter M Senge** The Fifth Discipline – The Art and Practice of the Learning Organisation, Doubleday NY 1990.

5. PREPARED TO LEARN

1 **Michael Keller Ditka, Jr.** (b.1939) Former American football NFL player and coach.
2 **John F Kennedy** (1917-1963) 35th President of America, assassinated in 1963.
3 **Publius Ovidius Naso** (43BCE–AD17/18) Roman poet.
4 **Arie de Geus** (b.1930) Former Royal Dutch Shell Executive. One of the world's leading corporate strategists & expert in organisational learning.
5 **Albert Einstein** (1897-1955) German/American physicist. Awarded Nobel Prize for Physics in 1921.
6 **Henry Latham Doherty** (1870-1939) American businessman & utilities expert.
7 **Baltasar Gracián y Morales** (1601-1658) Spanish baroque moralist, philosopher & Jesuit scholar.
8 **Benjamin Franklin** (1706-1790) A noted polymath & one of the Founding Fathers of America.

Notes

9 **Oliver Wendell Holmes** (1809-1894) American author & physician.

10 **John Dewey** (1859-1952) American psychologist, philosopher, educator, social critic & political activist.

6. PEOPLE CHOICE

1 **Arthur Ashe** (1943-1993) American tennis player. First African-American winner of a major men's singles championship.

2 **David MacKenzie Ogilvy** CBE (1911–1999) Advertising executive known as 'The Father of Advertising'. In 1948 with Anderson Hewitt, he formed Hewitt, Ogilvy, Benson & Mather, which became one of the world's largest advertising agencies.

3 **Ralph Waldo Emerson** (1803-1882) American transcendentalist poet, philosopher, lecturer & essayist.

4 **Knute Rockne** (1888-1931) Norwegian/American football player & coach at University of Notre Dame, South Bend, Indiana. Regarded as one of the greatest coaches in college football.

5 **Lawrence Peter 'Yogi' Berra** (b. 1925) Former Major League Baseball player & manager. Played almost his entire career for the New York Yankees. Nicknamed 'Yogi' as he was said to resemble a Hindu holy man when he sat around with arms and legs crossed waiting to bat.

6 **Robert Half** (1919-2001) Founder of Robert Half International recruitment agency.

7 **Frank Dick, Winning** – Motivation for Business, Sport and Life. Abingdon Publishing, 1992.

7. TEAMSHIP

1 **Sir Ian McGeechan** (b.1946) Rugby coach. Began career as player with 30 caps for Scotland. Coached Scottish national team & appointed head coach to British Lions on four separate occasions.

2 **Andy Roxburgh** (b.1943) Former Scottish football player & coach. Appointed UEFA Technical Director in 1994.

3 **Larry Bird** (b.1956) American former NBA Basketball player. Viewed as one of the greatest players of all time.

4 **Hendrik Johannes Cruyff** (b.1947) Former Dutch footballer & manager of Ajax and Barcelona. European Footballer

of the Year in 1971,1973 & 1974. Most famous exponent of the football philosophy known as Total Football.

5   **Ronaldo de Assis Moreira** (b.1980) Known as Ronaldinho. Brazilian footballer regarded as one of the most gifted footballers of his generation & one of few Brazilian players to have played at every international age level.

6   **John Robert Wooden** (1910-2010) American basketball coach. Member of the Basketball Hall of Fame as both player & coach.

7   **Sir Alexander 'Alex' Ferguson** (b.1941) Scottish football manager & former player. Manager of Manchester United since 1986.

8   **Abraham Lincoln** (1809-1865) Served as the 16th President of the United States 1861-1865. Gave Gettsburg Address & oversaw 13th amendment prohibiting slavery. Assassinated days after surrender of South.

9   **Joseph Rudyard Kipling** (1865-1936) British author & poet. Best known for works of fiction The Jungle Book, Kim & The Just So Stories. Awarded Nobel Prize in 1907. (From The Law of the Jungle, 2nd Jungle Book 1895)

10   **Oprah Gail Winfrey** (b.1954) American television host, producer, & philanthropist, best known for her talk show, which has become the highest-rated program of its kind in history.

11   **Vince Lombardi** (1913–1970) American professional footballl coach for Green Bay Packers & Washington Redskins.

12   **Michael Jeffrey Jordan** (b.1963) Retired American (NBA) professional basketball player notably with the Chicago Bulls. One of the most effectively marketed athletes of his generation instrumental in popularising NBA around the world during 1980's & 1990's.

13   **Ryunosuke Satoro** Japanese poet & author.

14   **Dan Topolski** (b.1945) Author, former rower & Oxford University's rowing eight coach 1973 to 1987 winning 12 out of 15 races during his tenure.

8. COACHWORKS

1   **Ralph Waldo Emerson** (1803-1882) American transcendentalist poet, philosopher, lecturer & essayist.

2   **John Robert Wooden** (1910-2010) American basketball coach. Member of the Basketball Hall of Fame as both player & coach.

Notes

3   **Ara Raoul Parseghian** (b.1923) former American collegiate football coach notably as the most successful Notre Dame University coach of the modern era.
4   **John Wooden** (see 2 above).
5   **Friedrich August von Hayek** (1899-1992) Austrian/British economist & philosopher.
6   **Jeanie Bergin** (b. 1959) Speaker & business consultant.
7   **Robert Nelson** (20th C) US author & speaker on management & employment.
8   **John Wooden** (see 2 above).

9.   PLANNING TO WIN

1   **Palmer, S.** PRACTICE: A model suitable for coaching, counselling, psychotherapy and stress management. The Coaching Psychologist, 2007, 3(2), 71-77, (page 75)
2   **Dembkowski, S., Eldridge, F.** 'Beyond GROW: a new coaching model', The International Journal of Mentoring and Coaching. (2003).
3   **Sir John Whitmore** (b. 1937) British racing driver & sports psychologist applying his skills to the world of business. Now a management consultant. The GROW model, originally conceived by Graham Alexander a ski & tennis coach & brought to the fore by Sir John Whitmore in 'Coaching for Performance' (1992) is possibly the best known model for coaching.
4   **Publilius Syrus** (1st century BCE) Latin writer of Syrian origin, sent as a slave to Italy where he was educated by his master.
5   **Alan Lakein** (20th C) American author on personal time management, including, How to Get Control of Your Time and Your Life.
6   **Mark Twain** (1835-1910) Pen name of Samuel Langhorne Clemens. American novelist & short story author.
7   **Lester R. Bittel** (b.1918) American author & internationally recognised authority on management and supervision.
8   **Boris Franz Becker** (b.1967) German former professional tennis player. Six-time Grand Slam singles champion, an Olympic gold medalist & youngest winner of the men's singles title at Wimbledon aged 17.
9   **Sun Tzu** (believed to have lived during the period 722–481 BCE) An ancient Chinese military general and strategist said to

have authored The Art of War, a book on military strategy considered a prime example of Taoist thinking.

10 **Henry Wadsworth Longfellow** (1807–1882) American educator & poet. (Quote from The Ladder of St. Augustine.)

10. PERFORMANCE DESIGN

1 **Confucius** (551-479 BCE) Chinese thinker & social philosopher.

2 **Vince Lombardi** (1913–1970) American professional football coach for Green Bay Packers & Washington Redskins.

3 **Marvin Phillips** (20th C) American author, broadcaster & motivational speaker.

4 **Mark Twain** (1835-1910) American author & humourist. Most noted for novels Adventures of Huckleberry Finn & The Adventures of Tom Sawyer.

5 **Brooks Robinson** (b.1937) Much acclaimed American former third baseman in Major League Baseball. Played 23 year career with Baltimore Orioles 1955-77.

6 **Michael Korda** (b.1933) British novelist & Editor in Chief of Simon and Schuster in New York. One of most influential people in publishing.

7 **Arthur Schopenhauer** (1788-1860) German philosopher known for his atheistic pessimism & philosophical clarity.

8 **Sir Winston Leonard Spencer Churchill** (1874-1965) British statesman & war leader. A notable orator and prolific writer.

11. FIGHTING SPIRIT

1 **William James** (1842-1910) Pioneering American psychologist & philosopher.

2 **Viktor Frankl** (1905-1997) Austrian neurologist, psychiatrist & Holocaust survivor. Founder of logotherapy a form of existential analysis.

3 **William 'Bill' Shankly** OBE (1913-1981) Player & one of Britain's most successful & respected football managers notably with Liverpool FC.

4 **Sam Ewing** (b.1949) American former baseball player.

5 **Gary Sinise** (b. 1955) American actor/director.

6 **Herm Albright** (1876-1944) Born Hermann Oliver Albrecht in Germany. Studied music and philosophy. Settled in San Francisco in 1905 & worked in publishing.

7 **Marcus Aurelius Antoninus Augustus** (121–180) Roman emperor & stoic philosopher.

8 **Joseph Rudyard Kipling** (1865-1936) British author & poet. Best known for works of fiction The Jungle Book, Kim & The Just So Stories. Awarded Nobel Prize in 1907 (Quote from the poem If).

9 **James A Belasco** American, business leadership strategist & author & **Ralph C Stayer** American corporate innovator.

10 **Roger Staubach** (b.1942) American businessman & legendary Hall of Fame quarterback for Dallas Cowboys.

11 **Ken Blanchard** (b.1939) American author, speaker & business consultant.

12 **Dan Topolski** (b.1945) Author, former rower & Oxford University's rowing eight coach 1973 to 1987 winning 12 out of 15 races during his tenure.

13 **Percy Cerutty** (1895–1975) Australian athletics coach. One of world's leading coaches during1950's/60's.

12. ADVANTAGE YOU

1 **Sallie Krawcheck** (b.1964) American business executive recognised in Forbes list of The World's 100 most powerful women.

2 **Dame Edith Sitwell** (1887-1964) British poet and critic.

3 **Mary Engelbreit** (b. 1952) American graphic artist & children's book illustrator.

4 **William Shakespeare** (1564 –1616) British poet & playwright, regarded as greatest writer in English language. (Quote from As You Like It).

5 **Martha Graham** (1894-1991) American dancer & choreographer, regarded as one of pioneers of modern dance.

6 **Steven Jobs** (b. 1955) American businessman, co-founder & CEO of Apple Computer Inc.

7 **Eleanor Roosevelt** (1884–1962) First Lady of the United States 1933-45.

8 **Henry Ford** (1863-1947) American founder of the Ford Motor Company.

9 **John F Kennedy** (1917-1963) 35th President of America, assassinated in 1963.

10 **Albert Schweitzer** (1875-1965) German/French theologian, musician, philosopher & physician. Awarded 1952 Nobel Peace Prize.

ADDITIONAL READING

1. E*
A Message to Garcia, Elbert Hubbard, Executive Books
This is my favourite little book that can be summed up very simply.
Just do it!

2. E*
Jonathan Livingston Seagull, Richard Bach, Scribner Book Company
The all-time great classic that lets you know that if you want to win;
if you believe you can win; and if you persistently fight to get there;
you win.

3. E
Like the Flowing River, Paulo Coelho, Harper Collins Paperbacks
It is worth taking time to go through what in effect is a collection of very
short essays of reflections. Not all may resonate – but most will.

4. E*
The Four Agreements, Don Miguel Ruiz, Amber-Allen Publishing
A very clear and simple approach to helping you shape how best to
live your values in pursuit of a better life.

5. E*
Fish, Stephen Lundin, Hodder & Stoughton
This is not a million miles from the thinking behind The Four
Agreements – but it offers a different four part framework that you
can relate immediately to the work place.

6. E
Who Moved my Cheese?, Spencer Johnson, Random House
An excellent, easy and enjoyable read that makes it really clear –
change is everywhere and it is the game to win.

7. E*
Purple Cow, Seth Goodwin, Penguin Group
This is a life changing book for those who have the courage to turn its words into effective action. It is about doing things differently and doing different things. It demands a new mind-set. It is a remarkable read about being remarkable.

8. E
The Big Moo, The Group of 33, Penguin Group
A fast good read with plenty of instant gratification from 32 writers providing one great parable after another.

9. R
Thinker Toys, Michael Michalko, Ten Speed Press
This is a great approach to helping you develop different ways of seeing things; and of thinking. It's jam packed with examples, ideas and exercises.

10. R
Blink, Malcolm Gladwell, Penguin Books
A good introduction to understanding the value of intuitive thought.

11. R*
Gut Feelings, Gerd Gigerenzer, Penguin Books
Taking the concept of intuitive thought and subconscious intelligence much further than 'Blink'. It is an outstanding read and a real nudge towards trusting your gut in doing the right thing. Trust sometimes means breaking the mould of conventional wisdom that says you must do things right.

12. E*
Beyond Winning, Gary M Walton, Leisure Press
The really great coaches, whatever their sport, have understood that they are not only preparing people for sport, but through it, for a better life. To do so they have seriously reflected on what a better life means for the person coached and/or that person to shape a better world; and the process of achieving this. The book is one of my major reference points as Gary Walton sets out the 'timeless wisdom of philosopher coaches'.

13. E*
Don't Die With The Music In You, Wayne Bennett, ABC Books
Great coaches not only prepare players or athletes and teams for their sport performance and competitive excellence, but through sport for a better life. This truly remarkable read epitomises this. It is less about winning in Rugby League than it is about winning in life's tough arenas. The book is bursting with message-soaked anecdotes and essential advice. A must read!

14. R
Winning Everyday, Lou Holtz, Harper Collins
A legendary NFL coach to Notre Dame College sets out a remarkably simple game plan to win in your arenas in life.

15. R
The Winner Within, Pat Riley, Berkley Publishing Group
Incredibly successful basketball coach to LA Lakers sets out an easily applied set of principles and guidelines to getting the best out of every player in your team.

16. R
When Pride still Mattered, David Maraniss, Simon & Schuster
Coaches have their role models – and amongst them Vince Lombardi – NFL coach to Green Bay Packers – is a god. This is the story of his life, his amazing success as a coach and how he influenced his players and staff to excel against all odds. It also sets out his key messages to business.

17. R
If You're Second You Are Nothing, Oliver Holt, Pan Books
A very illuminating insight into two great football managers – Bill Shankly and Alex Ferguson. This is less about comparing and contrasting as a revelation about two approaches to a winning attitude.

18. D
The Coach – Managing for Success, Ric Charlesworth, Pan Macmillan
Coaching one Olympic gold with a team is seen by most in sport as the achievement of a lifetime, so coaching a second team to achieve back to back gold's for Australia's 'Hockeyroos' is incredible. The

story of his personal journey; of addressing the issues that come with the dynamics of selecting and developing a team in an ever changing world of sport; and of meticulous attention to the technical business of preparing a world beating team while managing the people business of the persons involved is a master class for business and for sport.

19. R
Everyone's a Coach, Don Schula and Ken Blanchard, Harper Collins Publishers
Top NFL coach Schula (Miami Dolphins) and 'One Minute Manager' creator Blanchard bring sports coaching and effective leadership together.

20. R
What they don't Teach you at Harvard Business School, Mark McCormack, Bantam Dell Publishing Group
See below

21. R
What they Still don't Teach you at Harvard Business School, Mark McCormack, Bantam Dell Publishing Group
Very easily digested collection of excellent concise insights into real business situations and relationships.

22. R
First Things First, Stephen Covey, Simon & Schuster
A valuable overview of how to get what we do and how we do it in our busy lives – into perspective and into a sense of strategy for living life effectively.

23. E*
The VIP Strategy, Jim Clemmer/Art McNeil, Key Porter Books
Without a doubt this was the book that changed my whole perception of the world of leadership and people issues. It demystifies that world and gives you proactive tools to help you shape you, your team and your business in pursuit of achieving your goals.

24. E*
Top Performance, Zig Zigler, Berkley Publishing Group
Another big influence in helping me understand the simple truths

of managing relationships on the basis of getting the best out of yourself and your people. Pretty motivational too!

25. D
The Seven Habits of Highly Effective People, Stephen Covey, Pocket Books
This represents a truly great framework for every one of us who wants to get things done effectively – persistently.

26. R
The Way of the Leader, Donald G Krause, Berkley Publishing Group
Applying the principles of Sun Tzu and Confucius to modern business. Draws a lot on 'The Art of War' – a good 'makes you think' book.

27. E*
The Heart of a Leader, Ken Blanchard, David C. Cook Distribution
My personal opinion is that this book is Ken Blanchard's best; and the others are extremely good! He takes a quote on one page – discusses it on the next – then your head buzzes with what it means to you and how you can use it effectively. This is a great little book to dip into and out of and will make a difference every time you do so.

28. E
Winning, Frank Dick, Abingdon Publishing
Well I'd have to suggest this! These are the roots that fed the concepts we talk about when we get together. It is designed to help you be the best that you can be.

29. E
Winning Lines, Frank Dick, Abingdon Publishing
The idea here is to take time out to think differently about the journey from having a drive and dream – to delivery. A series of personal and collected one liners and quotes.

30. D
Re-imagine, Tom Peters, Dorling Kindersley
This is great reading for those who want to win the game of change by thinking beyond the horizon.

31. R

Giuliani Leadership, Ruldoph W Guiliani, Little Brown

Against the backdrop of 9:11, one of the most effective mayors of New York, who had already substantially transformed a city which had struggled to cope with crime and to serve its citizens, sets out a remarkable work on leadership. It is a great read and fascinating insight into how a leader learns and grows through the choices and decisions made in each experience that life throws up, whether under unbelievable pressure or not. Take time to work your way through. It has convinced me that there is no mountain you can't climb if you really want to get there and are prepared to do whatever it takes to get there.

32. R

Leader to Leader, Frances Hesselbein & Paul M Cohn, Jossey-Bass

There are 37 themes addressed by the greatest names and thinkers in leadership. It is one of those books you can pick up and get value from in a 15 minute read. Then return to it when for another 15 minutes from time to time until you get through it. Immensely useful.

33. R

The Future of Leadership, Randall P White, Philip Hodgson, Stuart Crainer, Ashridge

The fifth step in preparing to win is to rehearse extremes and change of pace. This is because, having got the technical and fitness bits in place, it is time to learn that life's toughest competition arenas are not flat water affairs! You must learn to excel in the white water stuff. In fact – you must seek it out! This is a fantastic preparation for such life.

34. D

Focus on Leadership, Larry C Spears & Michele Lawrence, John Wiley and Sons

My description of how we must see ourselves in our role within any corporate enterprise is as a 'player coach'. Editors Larry Spears and Michele Lawrence use a different term 'servant-leader' but the concepts are pretty close. Like Leader to Leader there are a series of 25 themes, all thought provoking. Although written for the USA market it is very relevant for anywhere in the world. You can dip in and out of this for 15-20 minute reads as you go back and forth through the themes. Each visit is worthwhile!

35. D

Developing Leadership Genius, Dr Cyril Levicki, McGraw-Hill Professional

No argument, this is a deeper book. This needs commitment in pursuit of a fuller understanding of the leadership development process. This is not to say it is a hard read. It is very readable. It goes deeply and comprehensively into the process and contains some pretty effective exercises. You must, however, be willing to go the full journey of the book with the author. If you do, you will find it very, very rewarding.

36. D*

Drive, John Viney, Bloomsbury

This is a fantastic book. It does, however, require that you take quality time to work through John Viney's brilliant study of what it takes to be a leader and how to remain one. It re-establishes management and the value of the entrepreneurial mind in the process. He lifts the lid on the highest quality leadership world and generates a real excitement to be a winner in that world.

37. D

The Fall, Steve Taylor, Natl Book Network

For such a complex subject matter this book is very readable and mind opening. It powerfully persuades the reader that humanity has volunteered itself, through our history into a psychological mess, yet asserts that we can also commence a journey to a more enlightened future. The book shifts the reader from a sense of foreboding towards real hope. The bottom line is that to effect the necessary changes of thought, attitude and action it is, as in all things in life, our personal decision that makes the difference. That is the situation whether we are talking of our personal behaviour, managing relationships or the natural environment.

38. R

The Last Lecture, Randy Pausch, Jeffrey Zaslow, Hodder & Stoughton

You would be excused for thinking this was going to be a heart wrenching read. After all Randy Pausch knew as he presented his last lecture at Carnegie Mellon University that he would be dead weeks later leaving behind a very young family. Yet, it is a celebration of life and as he puts it 'fulfilling your childhood dreams'. Truly inspirational.

Additional Reading

Key:
E = Easy enjoyable reading
R = Reflection needed reading
D = Deeper reflection needed reading
* = My essential reading list before working your way through the others

ABOUT THE AUTHOR

Dr Frank Dick OBE was educated at the Royal High School Edinburgh and Edinburgh University. He moved to Loughborough University to train as a teacher of physical education and mathematics and was later awarded a Fulbright scholarship to the University of Oregon. In 1970, he was appointed National Athletics Coach for Scotland and in 1979 became Director of Coaching for UK Athletics – a position he held until 1994. It was during his tenure that the UK athletics team rose to become a genuine power in world athletics, led by stars such as Sebastian Coe, Steve Ovett, Steve Cram, Dave Moorcroft and the double Olympic decathlon champion Daley Thompson, who coached by Frank, became one of the world's greatest ever athletes.

Frank has also used his expertise in coaching and training in athletics to benefit other sporting greats, including Boris Becker in tennis, Gerhard Berger in F1 racing, Katerina Witt in ice skating and Justin Rose in golf. Few coaches have successfully transferred their expertise across sports in this way and at such a high level. His book 'Sports Training Principles' was first published in 1980. Now in its 5th edition, this has become a classic multidisciplinary text book and was considered ahead of its time in applying science to sport.

Renowned as one of the UK's best and most consistently inspiring motivational speakers, Frank now combines his talent for world class sporting achievement through coaching in the business world. By recognising the synergy between effective coaching techniques on the playing field and in the commercial environment, he has developed a range of inspirational keynote themes, workshop topics and bespoke employee development programmes. His expertise derives from years of detailed research into individual success and achievement. Frank combines this wealth of knowledge and experience into an informative and motivational approach to achieving long-lasting transformation of both individual and team performance.

Frank is Chairman of Scottish Athletics, President of the European Athletics Coaches Association, member of the IAAF Coaches Commission, as well as Chair (and architect) of the IAAF Academy Management Board and is a board member of several other sporting organisations. His contribution to sport and coaching was recognised in 1989 when he was awarded an OBE. He was later inducted into the UK Coaches Hall of Fame and was given the prestigious title 'UK Sporting Hero' by Sport UK in 2001.